Tales of A "Greene" Possum Cop

By Bill Nance

I found "Tales of a 'Greene 'Possum Cop" to be a very informative, entertaining book. Mr. Nance has a folksy, engaging style and he really has a lot of good tales to tell!
— **Gail Ingram**
Principal, Towering Oaks Christian School

Bill has a way of drawing you into his stories. I'm glad he has taken the time to share some of his unique experiences as a wildlife officer in Tennessee.
— **Don King**
Chief of Information and Education
Tennessee Wildlife Resources Agency

Bill Nance spent 30 years roaming the woods, rivers and roads of Greene County in the line of duty. Two things never changed during all those years: his deep religious faith and his determination to do a good job in his chosen field. It won't take many pages of reading in this book to prove those points. ... told in a way that only someone with his down-home humor could do it.
— **Wayne Phillips**
Sports Editor Emeritus, *The Greeneville Sun*

I think you will enjoy reading these 'Possum Cop stories as told by an officer who spent over thirty years protecting the wildlife and citizens of Greene County.
— **Pat Hankins**
Sheriff , Greene County, Tennessee

Tales of A "Greene" 'Possum Cop
By Bill Nance

Copyright © 2014 by Bill Nance
Greeneville, Tennessee

ISBN-13: 978-1502944191
ISBN-10: 1502944197

Cover design and front photo by Bill Nance
Back cover bear photo by Phil Gentry
Chapter sketches by Sidney Holter, Kassidy Albert
Print composition by Richard D. Phillips

All Bible Verses are from "The Holy Bible," King James Version

Game and Fish, and Wildlife Resources shoulder patches used by permission of the Tennessee Wildlife Resources Agency.

Dedication

This book is dedicated to Steve Bowman, my fellow officer with the U. S. Forest Service. Steve and I swapped many stories and fought crime in and around the Cherokee National Forest for a number of years until he was tragically killed in the line of duty in a helicopter crash on June 24, 1998.

First I would like to thank our LORD and Savior, Jesus Christ, for His watch care over me and my fellow officers during the daily performance of our duties and especially during the times when things got a little "hairy." I thank Him also for helping me to hold my temper at times, be in control of the situation when necessary, and to present a positive image of Him and the Tennessee Wildlife Resources Agency to the hunters and fishermen of Greene County.

Over the years, many people have taught me, befriended me, put up with me, and otherwise contributed to my career of 30 years as a game warden/wildlife officer in Greene County, Tennessee. I am eternally grateful to all of these folks even though I can't thank each one of them individually. My Tennessee Game and Fish Commission/Tennessee Wildlife Resources Agency co-workers, the Greene County Sheriff's Department, the Greeneville Police Department, the Tennessee Highway Patrol, the United States Forest

Service, and law enforcement agencies from surrounding counties all played a big part in training me to be a productive game warden. These agencies allowed me to learn from their experienced officers, use their facilities, and borrow equipment when I needed it. Most importantly, they were always there to back me up in any dangerous situation just as I always tried to be there to help them when they needed it. I know I'm leaving out a lot of people, but special mention goes to Steve and Reed of the U. S. Forest Service; Clyde, Bill, and Rennie of the Greene County Sheriff's Office; Frank, Charles, Chuck, Mack, Bobby, Carl and Marcellous of the Greeneville Police Department; Don and Doug of the Tennessee Highway Patrol; and George, Mick, Ern, and all the District 1/Region TWRA 4 guys.

Special mention should go to the several Judicial Courts in Greene County and the First District. In the early 1970's, when I went to work as a game warden, many judges did not take wildlife violations seriously. Game wardens were sometimes laughed at and ridiculed for bringing violators into court. Even if a person was found guilty, the fine was small and usually suspended. The penalties handed down by many courts were certainly no deterrent to those who wished to violate wildlife laws. However, from the very beginning, I always had the support and cooperation of our courts, both General Sessions and Circuit. My first Sessions Judge Dan C. was an avid sportsman who knew the wildlife laws and understood the reasons for them. He also knew all the excuses that the accused violators would use to explain their actions. I don't think I ever lost a case in his court. His son has been a wildlife officer in a neighboring county for several years now. All the judges that presided over my cases took wildlife violations seriously and were not afraid to apply stiff penalties when appropriate. They made sure that they were knowledgeable about wildlife laws and their court decisions did much to deter wildlife violations in East Tennessee. Our courts were some of the first in the state to levy heavy fines and to sentence violators to jail time for wildlife violations. Many unethical "sportsmen" found themselves sitting at home during hunting season because their hunting privileges had been revoked by these dedicated judges.

Thanks also to my wife, Bonnie, for help in proofreading, selection of scriptures at the beginning of each chapter, and for lending a hand in just about every phase of writing this book.

Thanks to Wayne Phillips, Cameron Judd, Tom Yancy, Gail Ingram, Don King, Pat Hankins and Richard Phillips for help with proofreading, for writing teases, and for many valuable suggestions on grammar, syntax, and publishing.

Also, thanks to all the folks at Pine Springs Baptist Church for encouraging me in my feeble attempts to serve the Lord, for supporting me in the other things I try to do, and for all the excellent meals they have served me over the years.

A Note from the author

The tales in this book are true and occurred just as they are written with only a few minor changes to make the story read better. This book was not written to publicize my own career as a game warden/wildlife officer, but to give you, the reader, an idea of what it is like to be a law enforcement officer in Greene County, Tennessee. It was certainly not written to make fun of anyone or to embarrass anyone. I sincerely hope that no one is offended by anything he reads here. Violators are not specifically identified, although, in each tale, they were found guilty in court. Some were juveniles at the time and could not be identified by state law.

You may wonder why I have written about some events that have nothing to do with wildlife. As you will see, being a game warden/wildlife officer is a full time job. I always tried my best to put more hours into my work than was actually required. Almost everyone working in public service will end up doing that if they want to do a good job. However, you will see that there are not many wildlife officers in Tennessee, and to do even a decent job requires us to rely on other officers and the sportsmen for whom we work. We must cooperate with each other.

Therefore, when you read this book, you will see a little of what it was like for me to spend thirty years behind a badge and in the front seat of a green pick-up truck.

— Bill Nance

Contents

1

In the Beginning

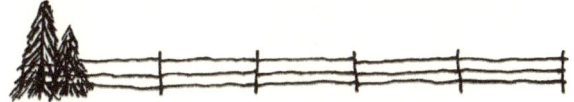

In the beginning,
God created the heavens and the earth.
Genesis 1:1

Southeast Texas was a good place for a boy to grow up in the
1950's. We were close enough to a big city to enjoy the Houston
Fat Stock Show and Rodeo each spring; at the same time there were
enough ranches and farms in the area to provide the wide open
spaces a young cowboy needed during his formative years. Other
than time spent in school, I was rarely inside the house except for
dinner (our noon meal). My grandmother always had a big meal
consisting of such country dishes as fried taters, butterbeans, fresh
tomatoes, cornbread, beef (or maybe an occasional goat roast), and
ice cold milk. During the summer, we might even have a dewberry or
peach cobbler for dessert. Then it was back outside to all the things
on the farm that can interest a growing boy. I would keep a close
eye on my granddad to see what he was doing and, as I got older, to

help him with whatever needed to be done at the time. Back then, it didn't seem like work to mow the grass, drive the International Cub tractor, or cut weeds in the pasture. Of course, there was the garden to look after and the chickens, the cow, and other livestock to tend. One of my assigned tasks was to keep the mockingbirds out of our fig tree. I don't know how good a job I did, but we always had plenty of fresh figs to eat and some left over to make fig preserves. They were right tasty on a hot biscuit.

During my high school years, I spent a lot of time hunting and fishing with my buddy, Charles. Dove hunting around the ponds in the cow pastures was always good in the fall. Rabbits were plentiful everywhere. Charles and I would rabbit hunt for a while after dark (it was legal in Texas) and then run a trotline in the bay for the rest of the night. When we got enough red fish, speckled trout, and flounder, we would invite friends and family over for a fish fry. It seemed like a good way to keep on the good side of everyone.

So you see, doing things indoors was never very high on my priority list. After my granddad got a television, we did enjoy watching rasslin' and "The Lone Ranger" on Friday nights, but that was about it. I didn't know it at the time, but I guess all these early years were preparing me for a career as a game warden. The Lord works in strange and mysterious ways.

After graduating from high school, I packed a few belongings and headed off to college with plans to become a chemical engineer. Now, I'm not sure why I chose that profession, but I had a cousin who was one, and growing up next door to one of the largest oil refineries in the world probably had something to do with it. It seemed like a good way to make a living and I thought I would be building chemical plants and such outdoors. Well, about five years later (it took that long for an engineering degree at my college) the big day arrived and I graduated with degrees in chemistry and chemical engineering. The next day, an old 1950 six-cylinder Chevrolet packed with a few clothes and a shotgun started me on my way about 900 miles northeast to Kingsport, Tennessee. There is a big ol' chemical plant there that offered me what I thought was a good job. Things went pretty well for a while but then I began to notice that being outdoors was not part of my job description. It seems that being an engineer with this company meant sitting in a small cubicle and thinking up things for other people to do. I was missing out on all the fun parts of the job.

Then one day, while I was picking up my mail at the post office, the Lord directed my attention to a notice on a bulletin board announcing that the State of Tennessee would be hiring ten or twelve game wardens for several counties across the state. Hmmmmm. That looked interesting to me and it had to be an outdoor job for sure. Wonder what it would be like to be a law man? I guess I could learn. The first thing was to send in an application with all my personal information and "qualifications". That done, it was just sit back and wait to hear from the state employment folks. Finally a letter came directing me to go to Nashville and take a test of some kind. I just thought that I was out of school. Okay. Test taken. Wait some more. Another letter came saying to go back to Nashville for a personal interview. I had no clue what to expect, but I put on my best coat and tie and went in to face the interview board. After everyone was introduced, I tried my best to act relaxed and to answer all their questions. They seemed satisfied and said "We'll let you know something." Wait some more. Around the middle of September, 1973, another letter arrived saying "You're hired and have second pick of the county you want to work in." Evidently the guy who had first choice took some other job so I picked first and chose Greene County because it was closest to where we already lived. A meeting with my soon-to-be captain was set up at the Johnson City office to make things official and get me started. He handed me a snub nose, aluminum frame, Smith & Wesson .38 special, told me to pick out a uniform shirt and pair of pants from the rack inside, and directed me to report to the Tennessee Law Enforcement Training Academy by five o'clock on Sunday afternoon. Thus began my career as a Tennessee game warden, or ranger, or rabbit sheriff, or wildlife officer, or 'possum cop. Take your pick. Six weeks later I graduated from the Law Enforcement Academy with a whole lot of new knowledge and a whole new life ahead.

Game & Fish Officer 113 is 10-8!

I got home from the academy on Friday afternoon and deer season opened in Greene County the next morning. So much for any time off. Sgt. George picked me up before daylight and we headed off into an unknown (to me) world to unknown places. Here went a really "green" game warden assigned to Greene County, Tennessee. Soon we arrived at a small, concrete block building heated by a kerosene space heater. This was the checking station for deer in Greene County. The space heater did little to warm the building on a very cold day, but I was all excited about the new job and the cold temperature made it feel like I was outdoors anyway. Sgt. George and the others were quick to show me how to fill out a harvest tag and how to take the required measurements from each deer. This was probably so they could get out and ride around instead of sitting in a cold checking station. The day passed pretty quickly and soon weighing deer, measuring antlers, checking teeth, etc. became routine. Finally, later that afternoon, I had my chance to get out and ride around with Captain Ern and Sergeant George. This was my first opportunity to actually check hunters in the great outdoors! I was also issued my official Game & Fish truck. O boy! My very own state vehicle to drive. A 1971, green, four wheel drive, Dodge Power Wagon! It even had decals on the doors, a spotlight, and a two-way radio. Now, I really felt important. No matter that I couldn't go anywhere by myself for three or four weeks. I could at least drive it home and park it in the driveway for everyone to see. Not long after the close of deer season (it was much shorter then), I was allowed to start getting out on my own and learning the county. I think that's when my game warden career really began. Learning the area, which included all the counties of the old District 1(Upper East Tennessee), and meeting the folks that I would be dealing with for the next thirty years quickly led me to believe that now I had a job which would be outdoors and very interesting. But, that begins the rest of the story.

2

Nolichucky Wood Duck Baptizing

*And there went unto him all the land of Judea, and they of
Jerusalem, and were all baptized of him in the river Jordan,
confessing their sins.* — Mark 1:5

That first winter brought a significant change in the organization
that is charged with protecting the wildlife of Tennessee.
Legislation was passed that changed the Tennessee Game and
Fish Commission to the Tennessee Wildlife Resources Agency.
The military ranking of officers was discontinued and we reported
to supervisors and assistant supervisors instead of captains and
lieutenants. Sergeants were eliminated. We became wildlife officers
instead of game wardens (we will always be game wardens to the
good citizens of Tennessee). Under the Game and Fish Commission,
we were required to work six days per week and couldn't be off
on weekends or holidays. Work days were sometimes twelve to
fourteen hours long. Under the new agency we were told that we
could occasionally take off an extra half day on Sunday if we went

to church. Later on, the work week was reduced to five days and the work day to a nominal eight hours. Of course, we were on call twenty-four hours a day, so this was not as big a change as it seemed. Not all changes that occurred with the new agency took place at once and some were years in coming. The Hunter Education Program did begin in the spring of 1974, and the agency began to place more emphasis on wildlife management, boating safety, hunter safety, and information/education. We were no longer just law enforcement officers; we had to learn many new jobs in a hurry.

That first summer saw my introduction to our wildlife management duties in the form of my first float down the Nolichucky River to count wood ducks. Officers George and Mick were my able tutors for this first trip. We put the fourteen foot john boat into the river just below the bridge on Highway 321. There is about a ten foot waterfall a few yards below the bridge so I was instructed to walk the boat around the fall near the river bank. When this was done, we all got into the boat with me in the front and George running the little Evinrude motor. Although it was early in the morning, the temperature was rising rapidly. It was already a hot day so we were enjoying the leisurely float while counting a few wood ducks and trying to determine if they were drakes or hens (eclipse plumage sometimes made this difficult). The little boat had not taken us far down the river when Mick spotted a hoop fish net up on the left bank. Because it was illegal to fish with hoop nets, we did the only thing good officers would do and motored over to the bank to investigate further. Since I was in the front of the boat, guess who had to get out to retrieve the net. I stepped up on the front of the boat and prepared to make a "short" jump to the river bank. To this very day, I'm convinced that Officer George backed the boat just far enough away from the bank so that I couldn't land in the grass and had to step onto the mud at water's edge. Did you know that river mud can be very slick? Even the new Browning boots that I had just been issued did not provide enough traction to keep me from rapidly sliding back toward the water. With cat-like quickness, I turned and grabbed the front of the boat, but it was too late. I don't know exactly how deep the river is at that particular spot, but it is at least neck deep. Yes, I was wearing a life jacket but it just kept me from finding out how deep the river really is. For the next few minutes, I tried to hold on to a violently shaking john boat while my companions rolled around on the bottom of the boat laughing. Finally they composed themselves enough to help me back into the boat and we proceeded with the duck counting. Actually the quick dip in a cool river on such a hot morning felt pretty good until I dried off. I don't remember how many wood ducks we counted but our data was probably somewhat inaccurate anyway. You see, I had trouble determining if I had heard a wood duck whistling or if my two boat mates were still chortling with glee over my "accident."

3

Too Early Turkey

Then they shall confess their sin
which they have done. — Numbers 5:7a

Along with deer restoration, turkey restoration has been one of the great success stories for wildlife management in Tennessee. In the early 1970's, except for a few small populations of wild turkeys on wildlife management areas, there were almost no wild birds in East Tennessee. Some attempts were made before I started working to stock pen raised wild turkeys, but success was extremely limited. Most birds wound up as tasty suppers for foxes, coyotes, bobcats, and anything else that could catch them. Probably more than a few ended up on dinner tables in the neighborhood.

After cannon nets and other live trapping methods were "discovered" by wildlife managers, the biologists decided that another stocking program should be attempted using trapped wild birds instead of pen raised ones. Techniques were perfected and soon some of the agency folks became quite efficient in catching these shy birds unharmed. An area with a trappable population would be baited with corn for several days until the turkeys were accustomed to gathering into a small area. Then the net was placed and baiting was continued to make sure the birds weren't afraid of the net. If everything went right (sometimes it didn't), early in the morning there would be a loud boom as the cannons fired the net out and over the feeding birds. If things worked according to plan, somewhere between four and twenty "big" black birds would be flopping under the net. After receiving a health check-up and a leg band, they were placed in specially designed transportation boxes and trucked to the release sites. I would get a call that the turkey guys were on their way with another load of birds. These first releases were always done in the most remote, wooded areas we could find because it was believed that wild turkeys would not survive too close to civilization. Boy, were we wrong. Using trapped wild birds worked great but they didn't have to be released into a wilderness. Now turkeys are seen in back yards, on carports, and anywhere else they can find something to eat.

We continued the stocking program for several years until there were just no other places left that didn't have a good population of birds. The number of turkeys grew almost exponentially until folks in the know said "now we can hunt 'em." Hunting seasons were set with limited hunting in most of the new areas, but, at least, we were going to see the results of our hard work. I think that one reason this restocking was so successful was because the sportsmen (and women), along with the general public were so cooperative in allowing us to stock birds on their farms and even babysitting them until they were well established. Folks were really protective of these "new" residents. It was best not to try to get your Thanksgiving dinner before the season opened or you were sure to be reported to the local game warden. We were sure to get a call with all the necessary information to apprehend the poacher. This cooperation, extra law enforcement, and stiff fines insured that enough turkeys survived for the first good hunt in a long time.

As opening day approached, the local newspapers all ran articles about the upcoming hunts. They wrote about the stocking program, gave tips on turkey hunting, and published the legal hunting dates for nearby areas. However one newspaper made a slight mistake. They gave the opening date as exactly one week before the proper date. That led to one of my first "big game" cases.

The phone rang on my day off and I thought, "Oh no. Here we go again. No yard mowing today." However it was Supervisor Ern telling me to meet a friend of his, a Mr. H, in the Sessions Judge's office at 9 o'clock the next day. It seems Mr. H had read the misprint in the newspaper and went turkey hunting a week early. Upon discovering his mistake, he called my boss and "fessed up" to his great sin. Now Mr. H was well thought of in his community; he was an honest, law abiding citizen with a squeaky clean reputation. Next morning, when I arrived at the judge's office, Mr. H was already there. "Hiz" Honor introduced us and Mr. H began his story. He was in the woods long before daylight and was nice and comfortable in his blind as the sunlight started to reach down through the trees. A few clucks on his handmade turkey call soon produced an answering gobble. Another cluck or two and here came ol' longbeard, just like he was supposed to. Boom. One shot and the hunt was over. On the way out of the woods, Mr. H noticed that there didn't seem to be any other hunters around. That was odd. Nobody at the checking station either.

"Uh oh! Something is definitely wrong. Better check some dates. Maybe I had better call my TWRA friend Supervisor Ern." At this point, Mr. H pulled the offending newspaper article out of his pocket and placed it on the judge's desk. Sure enough, the dates were printed wrong. My supervisor already knew what would be the proper action to take in this case, but I think he wanted to see if I could figure it out for myself. After a brief discussion with the judge (He was the best. I never lost a case in his court), he made it clear that if I charged Mr. H with anything, he would dismiss it. It didn't take me long to figure out that the proper thing to do in this case was nothing. I thanked the judge, thanked Mr. H for his honesty, and told him to let me know if I could ever be any help to him.

A few months later Supervisor Ern and I, along with our wives were invited to Mr. H's house for supper. I'm not sure exactly what the entrée was that night, but the dessert was a big sheet cake with a wild turkey drawn in icing on top and a turkey feather stuck in each corner. Ern and I were each given a handmade cedar turkey call. I still have mine. Mr. H continued to be a good friend to me and TWRA for many years. His family still is.

4

Preacher and the Turkey

Ye shall not steal, neither deal falsely,
neither lie to one another. — Leviticus 19:11

With the turkey season opening a week early for me, I was hoping for a nice, quiet real opening day. Alas, it was not to be. Since hunting in the Cherokee National Forest in Greene County would be open for the first time in several years, officers were brought in from surrounding counties to help work the hunt. We expected and got a large number of hunters from all over the area. Everything went smoothly for a while. Several birds were taken, and most folks seemed to be having a good hunt. One of the places that had a good population of turkeys and promised to be a productive area for hunting was Pine Mountain up above Pine Springs Church. A winding, almost one lane road, ran from the church up and across Pine Mountain and then down the other side to Paint Creek. About two thirds of the way up this road, behind the church, a large drain tile ran under the road to keep run off water from washing it out every time there was a hard rain. Being the ever alert and highly trained wildlife officers that we were, one of our guys checked the tile and, sure enough, there was something stuffed a couple of feet back into the down side opening. With the aid of sophisticated extraction equipment (a long forked stick), the object was fished out of the tile. Surprise! Surprise! A hen turkey (only gobblers were legal to hunt) wrapped in burlap lay before us. After quickly placing the deceased bird back into the tile, we devised a plan to catch the villain or villains who had committed this crime. It was a very complicated plan but almost sure to succeed. I backed my truck up a Forest Service trail above the tile into a place where I could see any vehicle that stopped to retrieve the ill-gotten bird. Another officer hid below the tile. We would have the crooks between us. No escape! Well, we didn't have to wait long. Forty-five minutes or an hour, at the most. Here came the vehicle we were looking for. It stopped right at the tile and two men got out. They spent several minutes calmly looking around and listening for other vehicles. Satisfied that there was no one watching them (except the unseen "Greene" warden) the little weaselly one crawled into the tile and came out with the bundle of burlap. His rather portly buddy was keeping watch for the wardens while the turkey was hidden in the back floorboard of their vehicle. With their "prize" now safely concealed, all that was left to do was to calmly drive out of the area and head for home. However, before the driver could start the engine, two green trucks magically appeared, one on each side of the poachers' vehicle. There was no place to go unless they wanted to drive off the steep side of the road and end up in the valley below in a very short time. They wisely chose to stay put. We quickly secured the scene and got identification from both men. The driver informed us that he was the Reverend Mr. C, pastor of a church in a neighboring county. The other man was Deacon G.A.C. of the same church. I guess he was trying to impress us or something. Normally, I try to be very respectful of our many fine ministers and certainly appreciate the good work they do. However, when anyone is caught in the apparent commission of a crime, I try to treat everyone alike. The appropriate citations were issued, evidence tagged, and the turkey confiscated (It went to feed the prisoners in the county jail). Thankfully, the rest of the day was pretty quiet.

This was my first encounter with these men but it certainly wouldn't be the last. It seems their reputation preceded them 'most everywhere I went. I arrested them a year or so later for possession of a firearm in a closed area. There were also "several" suspicious meetings over the next year or so.

Then, one day, Officer George got a call from Officer Lamar, our counterpart with the North Carolina Wildlife Resources Commission. He asked if we could come to federal court in Asheville for a trial involving a Reverend Mr. C and a Deacon G.A.C. They were charged with spotlighting deer on federal land in North Carolina. We were to bring all our court records pertaining to these two men because the honorable federal judge was very interested in their activities in Tennessee. The reverend and deacon probably expected only a short lecture and maybe a small fine. Why, they even had their high sheriff with them as a character witness. Imagine the look on the defendants' faces when two Tennessee Wildlife Officers with very official looking briefcases walked into the federal court room. Their attorney asked for a short recess while he conferred with his clients in the hall. Back in the court room, the learned counselor asked to approach the judge's bench. "Um, Your Honor, my clients feel it would be in their best interest to plead 'guilty' in this matter."

The long time federal judge stood up (not a good sign!), pointed a finger at the defendants and said, "YOU, THE REVEREND MR. C AND DEACON G.A.C., YOU'RE IN BIG TROUBLE!!! You were in my count just two weeks ago on the same charge. At that time, I was impressed with your church work and what fine, outstanding citizens you are. Now here you are back again. I AM NOT IMPRESSED THIS TIME!!! And you, Sheriff, how dare you come into my court and lie for these people." Talk about two guys sitting very still and sweating a lot. Officer George and I slipped out and headed back to Greene County before sentencing was complete, but wildlife violations in two states decreased noticeably for a while.

5

That Fish Caught My Rod!

*Now the LORD had prepared a great fish
to swallow up Jonah.* — Jonah 1:17

Sometime about the middle of my career, the Agency started placing more and more emphasis on boating enforcement and boating safety. That meant many more hours out in the broiling sun in an open boat instead of checking trout fishermen along a cool creek in the mountains. Those boats were air conditioned all right but not in the same way as my green truck. Also, since there are no big lakes in Greene County, we were on the road more, going from Cherokee Lake to Boone to South Holston. Officer George had been issued a boat left over from the World's Fair in Knoxville. It was a big, deep v-hull inboard/outboard, not fast but easier riding than some of the others. About the only comfort features we had were the air-ride truckers' seats. This was the boat I used most of the time and even assumed custody of it when Officer George transferred to Nashville. Boating enforcement meant many things. Besides the obvious duties like checking fishing licenses (see Chapter 20), checking boat registrations, checking personal floatation devices (life jackets to most people), checking running lights, and inspecting fire extinguishers; there were many other tasks to occupy our time. We taught boating safety classes, investigated boating accidents, assisted in drowning recoveries, provided traffic control for major events held on the water (see Chapter 23), and manned booths at boat shows. Most of our time was spent on the water though. We patrolled both day and night so folks knew they might be inspected any time they were out in their boat. One of the big problems for a while was night fishermen not wanting to burn the required lights after dark. This made them extremely hard to see and led to many unnecessary accidents. Then too, kind of like seat belts, lots of people just won't wear their life jackets. I could never understand why they wouldn't use something that could save their lives. Very few people who are conscious and wearing a personal floatation device ever drown. But enough of that sermon.

Whether day or night, most of our time was spent on routine patrol just checking to see if folks had their fishing license and were doing things safely. We usually didn't have to worry much about "over the limit" and such. There was no creel limit on crappie then, but after the size limit went into effect, we did have to be on the lookout for those who liked the little ones.

Cherokee is a big lake, touching four counties, if I'm not mistaken. We worked mostly Hamblen and Hawkins Counties because the other two were in a different area. I learned pretty quickly that there were lots of places to hide around a lake. We had to know the big hollows, the little hollows, the little hollows off the big hollows, the creeks, the boat docks (who had the best sandwiches), housing additions, bridges, and on and on. One of the fastest ways to learn our way around was give names to each hollow, landmark, or other familiar place. Some already had names: Three Springs, Turkey Creek, German Creek, Quarryville, and Panther Creek. Some we just named ourselves. The silos, the big island, Sycamore Lounge, Tennis Shoe Hollow. This last place was so named because we could usually find a number of locals bank fishing in the back of the hollow. Most of them wore tennis shoes so they could make a quick get-a-way if they saw the warden coming. Officer George and I were patrolling this area one hot day. Nobody was catching much of anything and we were mostly killing time until we could go home. Then we spotted a fisherman standing on a rock out in the water a few feet from shore. He was back in the hollow but the water was deep enough so that we could pull right up to him, check his license, and then head home. The man was very friendly and seemed glad to see us. He said he was fishing "fer one of them big ol' stripers" but hadn't even had a nibble all day. I asked to see his fishing license, anyway.

"Why shore, Mr. Warden. Got 'em right here." He placed his rod and reel gently on the rock he was standing on and reached into his back pocket to get the required paper work. Remember, I said the rock was out in the water a ways.

"Nice fishing rig," I commented as I checked his license.

"Yeah, I just bought it yesterday," he said, proudly. After I checked everything and assured him that he was legal, I reached to hand his license back to him. As he took it, his pole twitched. And then twitched again. All three of us just stared at it for a second. How he managed to stay on that little rock and bend over to grab his pole, I'll never know. He must have been pretty agile but he was just a tad slow. When he was about six inches from the rod handle, the whole rig disappeared in a microsecond. We saw a few bubbles about thirty feet out in the lake as the pole went straight down. Had to be "one of them big ol' stripers" that he was fishing for.

By the time I could mutter "sorry about that," Officer George had that Chevy I/O engine in our boat revved to maximum rpm and we were on our way out of the hollow and headed home.

6

Look, Ma! I'm on TV

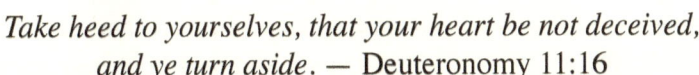

*Take heed to yourselves, that your heart be not deceived,
and ye turn aside.* — Deuteronomy 11:16

Besides calls about hunting without permission, I guess most wildlife officers get more calls about road hunting and spotlighting than anything else. Road hunting refers to a person slowly driving along back roads until some game is seen and then shooting it from either the roadside or from the vehicle. Both are illegal. In Tennessee, it is illegal to hunt from a vehicle except under certain conditions, and it is illegal to shoot on, onto, or across a public right-of-way. Spotlighting is, more or less, road hunting at night. A Q-beam or other high powered spotlight is used to locate the game, which is usually shot from the vehicle. During the daytime, the shooters will quickly leave the area and not return until they think they can retrieve their ill-gotten game without being seen. At night, the animal is rapidly thrown into the vehicle and then the fast driving starts. In most cases, the target is deer, but turkeys and, sometimes, other game are hunted too.

Sportsmen and legal hunters take a vastly different approach to their outdoor activities. They take time to study their game and its habits. They scout the area where they plan to hunt before the season opens to learn the game's movements and then prepare a blind, if necessary. These "good guys" study the hunting guide to make certain of season dates, open areas, bag limits, and any changes in rules or regulations. Sportsmen realize that legal hunting is a good wildlife management tool to help control over population and to weed out the weaker animals. Good hunters also prepare their equipment ahead of time to make sure everything is working properly and that they have what they need for an enjoyable hunt. Before opening day, a trip to the firing range hones their marksmanship and allows them to sight in their firearms. Always, always, permission is obtained from the land owner several days before going onto private property to hunt. Good hunters also leave everything on someone's property just as they find it.

The road hunter does none of these things. He's too lazy and greedy to exert any effort to do things the right way. He just wants his game as easily as he can get it. Road hunters and spotlighters are a problem both during open season and during closed season. It makes no difference to a thief when he steals. Years ago, some of these guys hunted for money and food. They would sell the meat and hides to get a few extra dollars or would take the meat home and eat it. That's not usually the reason for poaching nowadays. Welfare is even easier than road hunting. These folks just do it because, in their little minds, it is fun for them, and they think it makes them look big in the eyes of their friends. Since road hunters don't care about game or other people's property, they are not very careful where they shoot. The wildlife officer gets a call when they shoot toward cattle, barns, houses, and, yes, even toward people. Some folks also get sort of irritated when a big Q-beam lights up their bedroom at two o'clock in the morning. By the time the officer gets dressed (Even a good officer needs a little sleep once in a while.), drives ten or fifteen miles, and finds the right location, the thugs are usually long gone. Arrests under these circumstances are few and far between. Sometimes, officers might set up a work detail in a problem area. One officer (usually the rookie) will hide and watch the problem area while other officers will hide on either side of the watcher, ready to swoop down for the arrest if a violation occurs. Again success is limited and many sleepless nights are spent with no results.

One of the best tools to come along in the war against road hunters became available to us when somebody got the idea to have a taxidermist stuff a whole deer. The full mount could then be set up in a field frequented by deer to provide an opportunity for the poacher to do his thing more or less on command. Courts ruled that this wasn't entrapment; it was merely providing an opportunity to violate the law. The first mounts were pretty expensive so the Agency only bought one for each of the twelve areas across the state. They were passed around from county to county and were on the road more than they were out in a field waiting to take a shot from some greedy little road hunter. About this time someone named the deer "Timex" because he took a licking and kept on ticking. We couldn't use him very often but, boy, were we successful when we did. Then the U. S. Forest Service joined the fun and bought a couple of mounts for use in and around the Cherokee National Forest. We named them "Bucky." Thanks to Officer Steve, we now had access to these guys whenever we wanted them. Soon the mounts became more sophisticated. A couple of servomotors and a remote control allowed Bucky to flick his tail and to turn his head from side to side. The moving parts and a nice six point rack (never trophy size) proved to be irresistible to the road riders. At first we weren't allowed to use Bucky at night, but that changed after a while. You know, green reflective tape stuck on a metal post looks just like deer eyes in the beam of a spotlight. Now we could have a whole field full of deer with Bucky showing off out front for our would-be poachers.

Bucky and Timex made many cases for us across the state and here in Greene County. If it weren't for the fact that we were dealing with law breakers, almost every incident with the dummy deer proved to be, at least, a little humorous. Take the time Officer George was writing a man a citation for shooting at Timex. The man's young son kept pulling on his pants leg and saying, "I told you not to shoot him, Daddy. I told you not to shoot him." One of my more interesting cases occurred when Officer Steve, Deputy Rennie, and I had Bucky set up on Highway 107 in Houston Valley. A new TV station had just gone on the air in Greene County and they had a young cameraman/reporter name Danny who liked to film unusual happenings. He was also interested in law enforcement. We all got the idea that it would be fun to film someone shooting at Bucky. The muzzleloader deer hunt was going on so we set up Bucky in a good spot to watch and film the action. Sure enough, here came a slow moving pick-up truck. When it stopped, Bucky turned his head and looked at it. A couple of flicks of his tail was all it took. Two guys quietly got out of the truck, eased a big muzzleloader out of the back, and the younger one aligned the sights on Bucky's shoulder. A squeeze of the trigger and snap! The cap fired but didn't ignite the powder. The daddy grabbed the rifle from his son, put on a new cap, and drew down on Bucky again. Meanwhile, Bucky flicked his tail and patiently waited for the big boom from the charge of black powder. When the gun fired this time, Bucky just stood there watching the dumb hunters. About this time, our guys figured out something was wrong. They hurriedly threw the gun into the back of the truck, climbed in, and burned rubber for safer territory. What a show and Danny had it all on video tape! After a short chase, we found the truck parked in the driveway of a house a few hundred yards up the road, but nobody was in sight. A lady came out of the house and told us she didn't know the two occupants of the truck, but they both ran up the hill into the woods. Well, we had the truck and offending muzzleloader. All we needed were the two crooks. After much use of our public address system on our truck, threats to call in a police dog and even a helicopter, the daddy finally came out of the woods. That left only the grown son to round up. It seems he didn't stop running for ten miles until he got home. However Daddy persuaded him to turn himself in the next day. Boy, did my hand ache from writing all those citations.

After thinking it over, Daddy and son decided they would hire a lawyer and beat the rap in court. We honestly told the attorney that we had a video tape of all the action, but he didn't think we were serious since video taping crimes was something new at this time.

At the trial, we asked the judge if we could have a television set and video player brought to the courtroom. He agreed and, as we loaded the tape into the player, I noticed that our defendants seemed to be looking kind of pale. As the tape was playing, we could hear several audible chuckles from folks in the courtroom and especially from other attorneys. I think the judge even snickered a couple of times. When the tape was over, Mr. Attorney asked for a recess to confer with his clients. "Your Honor, my clients wish to plead guilty and ask for mercy from the court." It's hard to cross examine a video tape.

7

Drunk Tank Venison

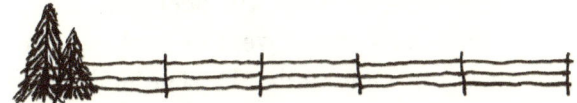

*And they did all eat and were filled; and they took up
of the broken meat that was left, seven basketfuls.*
— Matthew 15:37

One of the things that makes a wildlife officer's job so interesting is that we're doing something different all the time. Even the routine patrol is anything but routine. Each hunter checked is different. Each fisherman checked is different. Each hunter safety class needs to be taught differently. Each school program requires answers to different questions from the young students. Even each court case must be prepared differently and must be prosecuted using the unique evidence that has been collected. The long, hot days on the lake are usually filled with many different activities. We never knew when a family with a disabled boat might need assistance. Someone might catch a state record fish, or, Heaven forbid, there might be a boating accident that would require our full attention just over in the next cove. There could be injured people to help and the necessary reports to fill out. Never a dull moment. The long nights in a cold truck watching a field used by deer could prove to be interesting, too. We would try to find a good place to view the area where the poachers were plying their trade and that would also provide cover for the truck. We would make ourselves as comfortable as possible and then maintain radio silence (the poachers had scanners, too) for as long as necessary. All this might sound boring, but for those of us who enjoy the outdoors, night is a good time to be out. Deer would walk right up to our truck before they discovered that we shouldn't be there. A wary bobcat or bear might come for a short visit. We never knew what to expect. Then there was always the chance that the poachers would show up. Things would get really interesting in a hurry. Nothing routine now. I suppose you can see why wildlife officers enjoy their work and tend to put in many more hours than is required for the job.

However, there were a few things that I really didn't like doing. One of these was picking up road kill deer and disposing of the carcasses. For several years after I went to work, we were the only ones to do this dirty job. Thankfully, the state highway department began to give us some relief by using their front end loaders and dump trucks to provide much easier removal of the unfortunate road crossers. When we had to do it ourselves, it was usually quite messy and sometimes quite aromatic. A day in the hot, summer sun will ripen a dead deer in a hurry. Most of the time the driver of the vehicle didn't want the deer. Sometimes they didn't even stop or call about the accident. That meant we would not get to the scene until somebody notified us the next day. If the driver did want the deer or some other person wanted it, great! We could give them a receipt for it so that they could legally possess it. It was up to them to remove the animal and dispose of it. If we had to do it, there was usually a lot of dragging, lifting, and huffing and puffing involved. Then we had to find some place where we could safely dispose of the carcass. Not an easy thing to do. I won't go into much more detail. We just had to improvise.

One morning the Sheriff's department called to tell me that not one but two deer had been hit and killed on Highway 107 near the Nolichucky River bridge. Sure enough, when I got there, I found two big fat does that were DOA. Not in too bad a shape and fresh too. There was no one around so I huffed and puffed and finally got them into the truck. Now, what to do with them? They would make a lot of good venison so I hesitated to bury them or discard them somewhere. A call to the Sheriff's Department did not turn up any prospective takers but the dispatcher mentioned that they had a professional chef incarcerated in the jail. At that time we could give road kill to the sheriff's department to help feed the prisoners. After a quick call to the jail, the chef said, yeah, he could use them. It seems that this fellow was a very good chef and was called upon to cook for important visitors while he spent some time in the state prison. He met me at the back door to the jail and we decided that the drunk tank would be the best place to butcher the deer. We could hang them from the bars and there was plenty of fresh water to wash them down. The only problem was both drunk tanks were occupied. No big deal. We would just put the two prisoners in one tank and the two deer in the other one. The butchering was going well until we happened to notice that the two inebriated prisoners were turning various shades of green, yellow and purple. I think we discovered a new way to sober someone up in a hurry. I guess we should have informed them that drawing and quartering is not the usual punishment for being drunk. Anyway, the chef finished the butchering job, cut up the deer, and had them in the freezer in short order.

A couple of weeks later, I got a call to come to the Sheriff's Department about 12 noon or so but not to eat lunch first. The prisoners, the Sheriff's Deputies, courthouse employees and even a few passers-by enjoyed a noon feast of barbecued venison, green beans, buttered potatoes, homemade bread and banana pudding. I think we made a few friends around the courthouse with our "drunk tank venison" that day.

8

One Big Family

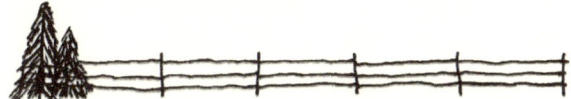

Fulfil ye my joy, that ye be likeminded, having the same love, being of one accord, of one mind. — Philippians 2:2

Please allow me to digress from my tales of a 'possum cop for this one chapter and talk about a subject that is very important to most law enforcement officers. The law enforcement profession, along with some other professions, is sometimes referred to as a closed society. "If you're not one of us, you might be against us." We have a language that is not easily understood by the general public. We might use words like "perpetrator" or "s.m.a.r. (semimonthly activity report)" or talk in ten codes. 10-4. 10-9 (repeat). 10-15 (have prisoner in custody). 10-42 (off duty at home). Some of our actions may seem a little strange to other people at times. Most officers do not like to sit with their backs to the door in a restaurant or other public place. We are also usually suspicious of people we don't know. "Wonder what they're doin' prowling around out here at this time of night. That truck sure looks suspicious. Better get the tag number." Even after fourteen years of retirement, I still sit with my back to the wall. I've been known to write down a few license plate numbers or descriptions of folks now and then. Never know what they might be up to. Most people are probably never aware of our "strange" behavior because it's pretty much an "in house" thing. All this is not necessarily bad. As a matter of fact, it's a pretty good thing. Law enforcement officers spend their careers looking out for the general public, but we are also very aware of looking out for our fellow officers. Due to the dangerous situations we must sometimes face, we have to be able to trust our partner to "have our back." I was lucky. I worked with officers that I could trust implicitly. Bill, Rennie, Clyde, Steve, Reed, Bobby, George, and many more. I hope they felt the same way about me.

When I went to work in the early 1970's, game wardens were not members of the law enforcement "society". They pretty much worked alone and kept separate from other officers and deputies. This may have been because, in some counties, other officers were sometimes the worst game violators (not in Greene County). Also, up until the last of my career, wildlife officers were not thought of as "real" law enforcement officers. Folks would look at us and exclaim, "Oh! YOU carry a gun!" Even my agency debated for a number of years over whether or not we had the authority to enforce laws other than game, fish, and boating laws. I always had plenty to do enforcing the wildlife laws and did not go out looking for other violators. However, if we saw a situation that was a threat to the safety of the public, we could, and usually did, try to do something about it. Sometimes my agency frowned on such activities, but I felt that I owed it to the people of Greene County to help keep them safe. But that's another subject.

Game wardens were assigned two to a county and, sometimes, only one to a county in my early days. That meant if we were to cover a big county like Greene, we rarely worked together and were pretty much on our own most of the time. Even if we were working at the same time, we could be separated by forty miles or more. If we encountered a dangerous situation, our fellow game warden might not be able to get to us in time to help simply because he was so far away. It didn't take me long to figure out that, if I needed help, it would have to come from the sheriff's department, police department or highway patrol. Therefore, it was extremely important to develop a good working relationship with them. I worked very hard to do that without neglecting my job as a game warden/wildlife officer. I tried to assure them that I would be there to back them if at all possible. If I were to be able to depend on other officers for help, they had to be able to depend on me. One big hindrance to developing a good relationship with the other departments, was that we had no communication with each other. Our radios had two frequencies, a car to car channel and a universal channel for communicating only with other wildlife personnel. With the sheriff's permission, I bought a radio on their frequency. It helped us tremendously. Deputies started reporting wildlife violations to me, and I would, in turn, alert them to situations that they needed to handle. Deputies, especially Bobby, even made several good wildlife arrests for us. Later the Greene County Court bought a portable radio with several frequencies on it and let me use it until our agency purchased more modern radios and portables for all wildlife officers. Now we could communicate with almost all departments and agencies. Our relationships and cooperation with each other got better and better.

In time, I was invited by the Greeneville Police Department and the Greene County Sheriff's Department to join them in many of their training exercises and in-service schools. I took advantage of these opportunities on my own time as much as possible. The classes weren't all wildlife related, but they all helped to broaden my law enforcement education and some proved to be extremely useful to our agency (as you will see in other chapters). The older, more experienced officers from all departments were always ready to let me learn from them. They never tried to tell me how to do my job, but they were more than willing to teach me what they knew. One might say "You need to be careful of that guy. He gives us all a lot of trouble." or "Better be alert when patrolling that area. We've had trouble there before." The Sheriff's Department was of invaluable help to me in transporting prisoners. Our vehicles were not equipped to transport dangerous people and, for a long time, we didn't even have handcuffs. I bought a set before I had been working very long and used them when necessary. Deputies were always prompt in coming to help me if I had someone in custody and needed to get them to jail. The Greeneville Police Department and, later, the Greene County Sheriff's Department even loaned me blue lights and a siren for my vehicle until my agency decided that we should abide by the state law for emergency vehicles. Once, when I was in town on my day off, I received word of a violation taking place in the Cherokee National Forest. The Greeneville PD shift leader said, "You don't need to answer that call without any communications," and then he handed me the keys to an out-of-service police cruiser. It's nice to have friends like that. Wonder what the folks on lower Paint Creek thought about a Greeneville police car checking people so far from home. My agency was also good about letting me attend various training classes that were available in East Tennessee. Walter State Community College and Professor Buster were super in letting me have access to their labs and equipment. After all this "schooling," I ended up being certified as an expert witness in General Sessions and Criminal Courts in firearms identification, firearms ballistics, hair identification, blood identification, fingerprint identification, chemical analyses, drug identification, and intoximeter operation. I was also certified in man tracking, emergency medicine, vehicle extrication, EOD (explosive ordinance disposal), hunter education instruction, boating safety instruction, and firearms instruction. I served as the agency's firearms instructor in East Tennessee for many years and was a certified Glock armorer during that time. In 1976, I was selected as Wildlife Officer of the Year for Region 4 and for the state of Tennessee and received the Shikar-Safari award for top officer. Like I said, always something different to do.

I fully realized that my job was to be the best game warden/ wildlife officer that I could be. I had more than enough to do without trying to be a policeman or deputy. However, just as an engineer can do a better job if he has a good working relationship with his equipment suppliers, salesmen, and assistants, I feel very strongly that we can all do a better job if we get along with those in similar professions. I know that I'm not the only wildlife officer that has a good relationship with other law enforcement agencies. Most of our people now get along very well with their coworkers. I was just lucky enough to be assigned to a county where we all cooperated with each other and could work to keep the good folks of Greene County and each other as safe as possible.

There were some fringe benefits to all this "big family" thing, too. One of the auxiliary policemen owned a restaurant and was a great cook (I'll bet you know where this is leading.). He also liked to get road kill venison or other tasty treats from me from time to time. Any Greene County officer was always welcome to stop by the restaurant on graveyard shift, occasionally, for a meal of venison stew, oyster stew, cornbread, pie, etc. I think we even had a "secret code" to let everyone know when supper was ready. A cafeteria owner and his wife were also good friends to officers and always made us feel welcome at their place of business. She surely could make good coconut pies and blackberry cobbler. The Greene County Officers' Association picnics were always well attended because of all the good cooks we had. Yes, most officers like to eat. We sometimes missed a meal in the line of duty so we had to make up for that when we could.

We had many good times during the thirty years that I was "on duty." There were some sad times, too. A couple of officers lost their lives in the line of duty while I worked. Several others passed away rather unexpectedly. It was never easy to lose someone with whom you worked closely. However, I think the strong faith of some of the officers made things easier for everybody. Just like any family, there were ups and downs, good times and problems, but I'm just thankful that I had the chance to spend my career working with this big family in Greene County. Now back to the 'possum cop tales.

9

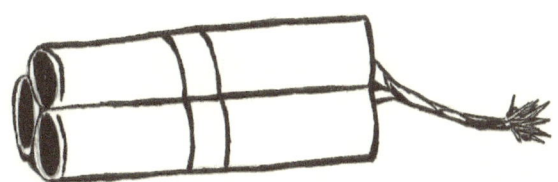

Dynamite and Little Trout

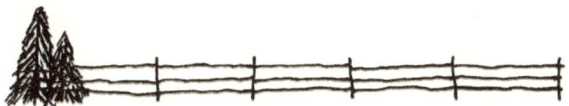

The voice of thy thunder was in the heaven:
the lightnings lightened the world: the earth trembled and shook.
— Psalm 77:18

No, this chapter is not about illegal methods for taking fish. It is about a potentially dangerous situation that occurred at the Erwin Trout Rearing Station operated by my agency. Most people call it the trout hatchery, but that's not really correct. Small fingerling trout are trucked to the rearing station and placed into long raceways. They are then fed a "fast grow" diet until they are big enough to be stocked into area streams and lakes. The guys who take care of these little trout do a great job and provide many hours of recreation for East Tennessee fishermen. Not to mention some mighty tasty suppers.

As I mentioned in the last chapter, one of the in-service classes that I took with other local officers was an explosive ordinance disposal course. It consisted of two, one-week sessions, taught at two different times. Both sessions were taught by EOD teams from the 101st Airborne Division stationed at Fort Campbell, Kentucky. We met on campus at East Tennessee State University in the student union building. You can imagine the looks we got from students and faculty when thirty or thirty-five guys in full dress army BDUs (battle dress uniforms) and wearing full duty belts came trooping into the student union each morning. If that weren't enough, next came the EOD team carrying crates of TNT, C-4, det cord, grenades, bombs, and other goodies. We spent half a day in the classroom and, then, went out to the landfill in the afternoon and blew up lots of things like cars, trees, railroad rails, and old explosives from departments around East Tennessee. Boy, did we have a good time for those two weeks. As a final exam for the course, the EOD team "mined" the cafeteria in the basement of the student union with grenade simulators and artillery simulators. They set up trip wires and other triggering devices in such a way that they were sure we wouldn't find them. Our job was to go in and clear the building of any unsafe devices without setting off any of the simulators. Now these simulators were as loud as the real ones, but they just didn't have any destructive force. As you might guess, we found all the simulators and didn't set off a single one. Our instructors were somewhat disappointed that they hadn't fooled us so they kicked a few trip wires just for the fun of it. The whole student union shook for about five minutes. We quickly got the attention of the campus police and everyone in the building. They thought anything from an air raid to an earthquake had taken place. We probably couldn't get away with anything like that nowadays, but it sure was fun.

A few weeks after this class was over, the agency hired several new wildlife officers. One of them, Officer Pete, was assigned to Unicoi County. Since Pete was young and single and he hadn't had a chance to find a place to live, he set up a cot in the storage room of the Erwin Trout Rearing Station. It was warm and dry and had a kitchen and a shower. All the comforts of home except for Mama's cooking. We were talking one day and something came up about the EOD class. Officer Pete casually mentioned that there was a case of dynamite in the storage room next to his bed. It appeared to be rather old and probably hadn't been opened in quite some time. Because of what we had just learned in our class, this information raised a big red flag with me. "Pete, let's go look at the dynamite, NOW!" Just as he had said, there it was, a cardboard box about 3 x 2 x 2 feet labeled "Austin Powder Company – Nitroglycerin Based Dynamite." As almost any chemist can tell you, nitroglycerin is somewhat unstable in liquid form, and highly unstable in crystalline form. Usually it is mixed with sawdust, cotton or other material to make it safer to handle and then rolled in wax paper to produce sticks of dynamite. A quick check with some of the older employees told us the box was probably left over from construction of the raceways and ponds necessary for rearing the trout. That meant it had been there for quite a few years. Since gravity always is at work, the nitro will usually leak out of the sticks of dynamite and run down into the bottom of the box. There it will crystallize and become VERY unstable. A slight bump, jar, or ever a small earth tremor could detonate it. To make matters worse, there was a full one thousand gallon gasoline tank attached to the building. Several people's lives and a lot of state property were in immediate danger.

"Pete," I said, "I believe we had better find you another bedroom until we can take care of this situation." After I secured the storage room and made sure all employees knew to stay away from it, my call to the regional office was answered by the assistant regional manager. This situation was something the agency had never dealt with before and there were no guidelines covering dynamite removal. With all due respect to the assistant regional manager's position, I carefully explained the circumstances and tried to assure him that I could handle the removal and make the rearing station safe for the little trout. I'm not sure he was convinced that I knew what I was talking about, but he finally agreed to let me take care of everything. Lest you think that I have a high opinion of my abilities, my next action was to place a phone call to Ft. Campbell and asked to speak to the sergeant who taught our EOD class. A quick description of our situation was all the sergeant needed. He knew exactly what we had. After consulting with his commanding officer, he said "We'll have an EOD team on a helicopter headed your way by 9:00 a.m. tomorrow morning." Sure enough, they arrived by noon the next day and we drove them from the landing zone to the rearing station. The sergeant carefully examined the box without touching it and then slowly removed the lid. "Hmmm. That's good and that's bad," he said. The box had a plastic liner that actually contained the dynamite. That's good. The liner kept the nitro from soaking into the cardboard bottom and into the floor. If that had happened, the EOD team's advice would have been to burn down the building. Not a popular option. However, the bad news was that the sergeant could see nitro crystals in the plastic liner.

His comment this time was, "I'm not sure if we can move it."

"But Sergeant, didn't you tell us that antifreeze (ethylene glycol) could be used to soften and desensitize nitroglycerin crystals?"

"Well, yeah. That might work. Got any?"

"Sure. There's plenty here in the building. They use it all the time." Okay! Carefully the sergeant cut a small hole in one corner of the plastic liner. I held the funnel and he poured the liner level full of antifreeze. Then we waited for an hour or so to let the antifreeze work.

After about ninety minutes, the sergeant said "Well, let's do it." and sent everybody else out of the building. Then he bravely (and carefully) picked up the box of dynamite, carried it outside, and placed it into the bed of Officer Pete's brand new shiny green pickup truck. We had previously put several layers of blankets into the truck bed for cushioning and, then, we put some more blankets over the top of the box to keep anything from sliding around. The sergeant crawled up into the truck and sat down with the dynamite between his feet. "Okay, let's roll!"

Before we left the rearing station, I called the regional office to advise them that the rearing station was now clear and safe. I also called the Erwin Police Department and the Unicoi County Sheriff's Department to let them know that we would be transporting some hazardous materials away from the rearing station. I led the way because I had the only truck with blue lights. Next came the truck with the dynamite and, finally, another truck as rear guard. We drove up into a remote section of the Cherokee National Forest at about five miles per hour, if that fast. The few people we met were told that, because of official Government business, they had to vacate the area for the rest of the day. Some were heard spreading a tale that

"The gov'mint's up to somethin' big up on the mountain. We think its nook-u-lar!" About two hours later, we came to a high, remote hilltop and decided that would be a good place to "dispose" of the dynamite. Three or four blocks of C-4, some wraps of det cord, and a couple of fuse caps, and we were all set. A two minute countdown began. Then 5, 4, 3, 2, 1. BOOM!!!! It was all over, but it probably did sound like "somethin' nook-u-lar" to those folks down below. Twenty minutes later, we were back at the rearing station enjoying a cold soda and thanking the guys from the 101st Airborne. As their helicopter rose and turned toward Ft. Campbell, we could look back on just another day in the life of a game warden. I sent a detailed report of exactly what took place to the Nashville office but never got a reply back. I guess they thought dynamite removal was all in the line of duty for a Tennessee wildlife officer. At least, Officer Pete had a safe bedroom once again. Just for you, Pete, thanks for my "Sarge."

A few weeks later, a similar, but totally unrelated incident occurred when I got a call from the Sheriff's Department. It seems that a man who lived out on Horse Creek phoned them and said that he had found some old grenades in a World War II Navy foot locker. He just wanted to get rid of them and asked for a deputy to come get them. I guess the Sheriff's Department's EOD man was off duty that day so they called me. This didn't seem like a real big deal. World War II pineapple grenades are fairly easy to disarm and they do make good paper weights. Maybe I could hang on to one or two for souvenirs. When I drove up to the man's garage, he went in and came back out with a large paper sack. He dropped it on the ground in front of me and said, "There they are." Being much more careful than this gentleman, I gently opened the top of the bag. What I saw inside was definitely not U.S. made pineapple grenades. They looked like cans of c-rations with detonators on top. With the aid of a flashlight, I could see some markings on the sides of the cans. These markings were not in English and were unreadable beyond the fact that they were distinctly oriental. OK! Time for re-enforcements once again. A phone call to the Greeneville Police Department got me in touch with Officer Mack, their EOD man.

"Stand by!" he said. "I'll be there shortly." Upon arrival, Officer Mack made the same, careful examination I had made and, pretty much came to the same conclusion. The items in the bag appeared to be some type of Japanese mortar-launched grenades. Now, toward the end of the war, the Japanese used many different explosives in their ordinance. Picric acid, black powder, or just about anything that would blow up. We really had no way of knowing what we had except that the grenades seemed to be in pretty good shape with very little corrosion. Officer Mack decided to take them back to Greeneville and call the 101st Airborne guys again. As Officer Mack described the grenades to them over the phone, we could hear them squealing with delight. It turned out that our "souvenirs" were, indeed, Japanese mortar-launched grenades. "We need them for our training classes. We'll be right there to pick them up." Sure enough, a few days later, a green army truck rolled up, two EOD men got out and grabbed our sack of grenades. "These are the best examples of Japanese ordinance we've ever seen," they exclaimed. They thanked us, shook hands, and headed to Fort Campbell with my "paper weights." I guess they were, at least, put to good use.

10

Coon Huntin' Preacher

And it shall be, when he shall be guilty of one of these things,
that he shall confess that he has sinned in that thing.
— Leviticus 5:5

When I went to work in East Tennessee, raccoons were about as scarce around here as timber wolves and black panthers (No, we don't stock either of these.). As much as we worked nights, I think I only saw two coons that winter. Both were in the Cherokee National Forest. Since coon huntin' is almost a religion to a lot of the mountain folks, some of them decided that something just had to be done. This usually meant buying raccoons that were trapped in other states and releasing them locally where they could be hunted later. This could be done either legally or illegally. Importation of raccoons from several states is illegal because these states have a high number of coons with rabies and other diseases. Even when the raccoons were brought in legally, they had to be vaccinated for rabies, parvo, distemper, and such before they could be released.

The agency provided this veterinarian service to the coon hunters at no charge. This was done as a protection to the native raccoons and to domestic animals that can contract the same diseases. However, many coons were still brought into Tennessee illegally and these posed a big problem for us. Not only were we kept busy trying to catch the illegal importers, we also had our hands full trying to keep other folks from killing the coons out of season. For several years, coon hides sold at a high price on the fur market. One group would bring in a bunch of raccoons, and another group would kill them and stretch their hides. The hunters would tell on the poachers, but the poachers wouldn't tell on anybody because they wanted more coons to kill.

This all went on for several years. We would catch a few importers, but many more "got away." Finally, the price of fur dropped low enough that it was hardly worthwhile to poach any animal for its hide. Some of our "headaches" had to find other ways to supplement their income. The result of bringing in so many raccoons was that the coon population increased very rapidly over a period of a few years. At first, most folks enjoyed seeing the furry little bandits in their backyards and around their farms. The coon hunters could usually count on treeing at least a couple of coons on any given night. You would think that now everybody would be happy, but not so fast. The little ringtails began to wreck people's gardens, eat their cat food, tear holes in their grain sacks in the barn, and to otherwise make real pests of themselves. Instead of getting calls about people poaching coons, wildlife officers were now getting calls wanting something done to reduce the coon population. Raccoon depredation continues to be a big problem in many areas. It is not unusual for a farmer to catch seven or eight raccoons in the same corn patch in just a few nights. In most cases these wayward animals are released in remote areas where they will, hopefully, stay out of trouble. If they don't all get run over on the highways, coons are probably here to stay.

Around these parts, coon hounds are serious business to a lot of folks. Many times, they're part of the family. A man knows his coon hounds as well (or better) than he knows his kids. Good dogs are a source of pride to their owners. If you can't brag about your dogs, why have them?

"Yep, that's ol' Buck out front. Rattler's not fur behind and ketchin' up fast. Now they're treed. Best go shake thet ol' coon out so we kin watch the fun." If the hunters were lucky enough to tree a coon instead of a 'possum or skunk, the story would be retold many times in the next few days. In my early years, in order to protect the resource (raccoons), we had a pretty short taking season in East Tennessee. That all changed as the population of raccoons continued to increase. In order to make up for the short taking season, the agency allowed coon hunters to "train their dogs" at other times during the year. That is, they could chase a coon, but they weren't supposed to kill it or be in possession of a firearm. Theoretically, a training season should work well and still protect the raccoon. The dogs would get some exercise, young dogs could learn from the older dogs, and everyone could enjoy the "music" of a good chase. Unfortunately, things didn't always work out that way. There were always some folks who just couldn't be content with catching their dogs and leaving the coon up the tree.

That's where we came in. A two o'clock phone call saying, "Mr. Warden, they're at it again. Yeah, the same ones as the other night. Just shot twice up on the ridge behind the barn." Get dressed, fire up the green truck, and here we go again. Most of the time, the hunters were gone when we got there, but occasionally we would find their truck and then, hide and wait. I usually would try to get out sight but not out of hearing. Dogs make a lot of noise when you're trying to catch them and load them into a small box in the bed of a pick-up. If they had a coon or gun, the case was pretty well decided at that point. However, if there were no coon or gun, we had to work a little harder to determine if a violation had occurred. Did they hide the gun in the woods until after they were sure there were no game wardens around? Maybe they would hide the coon and come back to get it later. One favorite trick was for one person to come to the truck and to start catching and loading dogs. The others would stay hidden in the woods until they were sure it was "safe" to come out. If the warden showed up, he would find only one hunter and no coon or gun. The guys in the woods either walked to a prearranged place for pick up or someone came back to get them later.

This is just what happened to me one night. I got the call, dressed, and headed to the scene. Sure enough, there was the truck with the dog box in the back. I parked out of sight just over a little rise in the road and waited. After thirty minutes or so, I heard the dogs barking and the clatter around the truck so I closed in with blue lights flashing like any good officer. You guessed it. There was only one hunter at the truck. "Nice night to train your dogs, isn't it?"

"Yes, sir, Mr. Warden. Had a good chase but I got to work tomorrow so I'm on my way home." After an inspection of the truck and surrounding area, I was unable to find a coon or gun. A quick count did turn up more dogs than one man would probably have. There were one pair of muddy boots and two pairs of clean shoes in the truck. Two jackets that wouldn't be worn for hunting were also in plain sight.

"Sir, you might want to call your two friends out of the woods so we can take care of this matter before it gets any later." After a little coaxing, the two other hunters decided to "give up" and come to the truck. Still, there was no coon or gun. Each had his license (required even for dog training). Everything seemed to be in order, but something just didn't feel right. I wrote down everyone's name, address, phone number, and where he worked. I don't remember where one man worked, but one owned a pawn shop and the other was the pastor of a local church. There's certainly nothing wrong with being a coon huntin' preacher. Lots of pastors like to hunt. It's a good, clean sport. All the men were polite and friendly to me. There were no problems at all. I thanked the men for their cooperation and we drove off in different directions. Still, I just had that feeling that I was missing something. Guess it wouldn't hurt to go back and take another look around. I parked where the hunters' truck had been and walked up into the woods. My big Maglight flashlight lit up the world around me. About half way up the ridge, I saw something that didn't look like it belonged in the woods. A small bag of some kind. I picked it up and opened it. Now, what would a bag of .22 cartridges be doing out here in the woods? Some more searching turned up nothing. I was just about to give up when my Maglight reflected off of something shiny. Leaned up against the back side of a tree was a .22 caliber rifle. It was still warm from being carried under a coat.

The next day, I stopped by the pawn shop belonging to one of the hunters. When he was alone, I showed him the rifle and asked if he had ever seen it before.

"Yeah, I have. It's my granddad's gun. If I pay the fine, can I get it back?" I assured him that he could do just that and issued the necessary citation. The other two hunters met with me the next day and were issued their citations. They weren't mad at me and I certainly wasn't mad at them. I appreciated their good attitude and told them so. We, like everyone else, just have a job to do. The good pastor (and he is a good pastor) was a little worried about what his congregation would think so I assured him that they would not find out about what had happened from me. However, someone told me later that he made a full confession to his congregation the next Sunday. As the Good Book says, I guess confession is good for the soul.

11

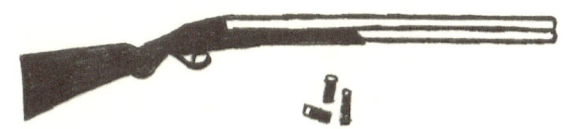

Can I Shoot Again, Please?

Be strong and of good courage; be not afraid,
neither be thou dismayed: for The LORD thy God is with thee
whithersoever thou goest. — Joshua 1:9

Not long after the Tennessee Game and Fish Commission became the Tennessee Wildlife Resources Agency, a very important program was initiated. This was the Hunter Education Course or Hunter Safety Course. The names are used interchangeably and refer to the same program. The agency was given the responsibility for setting up and administering the course and for certifying instructors to teach the classes. The first instructors certified were the state's wildlife officers. That was over forty years ago. At first, participation in the program was voluntary, but the classes proved so popular that they were filled to capacity with both juveniles and adults. Responsible adults who were not employees of the agency could also be certified as instructors by completing a training class, completing the student class, and assisting in teaching a class. These "volunteer" instructors were extremely important in making classes available to all those who wanted to take them.

A few years later, legislation was passed that made graduation from a certified hunter education class mandatory for some hunters. As the law stands, everyone born on or after January 1, 1969, must complete the course and carry proof of completion with them in order to legally hunt in Tennessee. Now the agency had to make a hunter education class available to anyone who needed to take it. Once again, the volunteer instructors were key in helping to certify so many hunters so quickly. Many hunters and sportsmen (women, too) who believed in the program became certified instructors and taught classes that wildlife officers just didn't have time to teach. In Greene County, we have been blessed to have many dedicated volunteer instructors from the time the program first started. Early on, I contacted the Greene County School Board and the Greeneville City School Board to see if they would be willing to let us teach the course during school hours as part of the physical education classes. It seemed to me that a good way to make hunter education available to the young people who were required to take it, would be to offer it in the schools. Both school boards not only gave their okay, but whole-heartedly supported the idea. Soon we had physical education teachers in several schools certified to teach the classes. Most of them were hunters and sportsmen and really enjoyed teaching something they believed in. The kids welcomed the break from "regular" school work and couldn't wait to sign up for a class.

The course consists of instruction in wildlife conservation and laws, firearms identification and mechanics, archery, black powder and muzzleloaders, survival and first aid, ethics, wildlife management, home safety, and field safety. Students are required to pass a written exam with a score of seventy-five out of a hundred. Last, but not least, they must demonstrate their knowledge and ability to handle a firearm safely in a live firing exercise. In Greene County we mostly used semiautomatic shotguns and shot at moving clay targets. The students are not graded on marksmanship, but only on how safely they handle the shotgun. Failure on either the written exam or the live firing exercise means the student must repeat the entire course. We want participants to enjoy the class but they must also understand that handling a firearm is a serious matter. In all the years that I taught hunter education, I don't think I had more than one or two people to fail the live firing exercise. Although I probably certified several thousand graduates of the hunter education course over my career, I don't remember ever writing a citation to one of my former students.

Now, back to my hunter education tale. As I mentioned, many classes taught in the schools were taught by certified school teachers. However, if there were no certified teachers at a school, the wildlife officers would teach the class. Such was the case at one of the Greene County high schools several years ago. After I briefed the principal on the course, he readily gave his okay for me to teach a class during one of the physical education periods. With the help of the P.E. teacher, we got all the projectors and equipment set up (no dvd's back then) and started the class. Everything went well. The students were interested and eager to participate in our demonstrations and hands-on instruction during the class time. Everyone passed the written exam with flying colors and we scheduled the live firing exercise for the next day. By class time, the trap thrower was set up, the shotguns were arranged, and all was ready for the students. After we demonstrated the proper operation of the shotgun, the proper stance, and the firing procedure, the teacher lined up the class to begin the live firing. For safety reasons, the students shot one at a time. After we gave them a shell and helped them to load, if necessary, the shooter would yell "pull" when he wanted the clay target thrown. When he thought he was lined up on the moving clay bird, he could squeeze the trigger and, if he did everything right, break the target. While helping one student, I happened to notice a young lady a few students back in the line. She was obviously quite nervous and apprehensive about taking her turn. By the time she got up to me, tears were running down her cheeks and she just wasn't sure she could "do this." A few assurances that everything would be all right and that she wouldn't be hurt calmed her down a little bit, and she decided that maybe she could do it after all. Although she was still shaking quite a bit, we got her into the proper stance, got the shotgun loaded, and she was ready.

"Pull!" "Boom!" One clay target reduced to dust. See that wasn't so bad, was it.

Sob. "No".

Okay, let's try another one. "Pull!" "Boom!" Same result. Powdered target. Hmmm. Very good. Now, one more and you're done.

"Pull!" "Boom!" Three in a row! I complimented the young lady on a job well done and moved on to the other students. Back then, if we had time after everyone had finished shooting, and if we had a few extra shells, we would let some of the kids shoot again. Guess who was first in line wanting to shoot some more. Three more shots, three more broken clay targets, and a grin as wide as the goal posts down on the football field made all the effort I had put into the class worthwhile.

Even though this young lady was scared to death, she listened to her instructors and tried to do things the right way. She proves that the hunter education courses are working. Since the first Hunter Education class in Tennessee was taught some forty years ago, approximately 715,000 graduates have been certified as safe hunters. In the year 2000, Tennessee's course was named the top hunter education course in North America. No doubt, many lives have been saved because of the dedication and hard work of Tennessee's wildlife officers and volunteer instructors. Thanks to all of you!

12

Just One More Deer Tonight, Boys

Thou shalt not steal. — Exodus 20:15

Poaching is stealing! Poaching is the illegal taking of game animals. It has been a problem since medieval days when the kings owned all the land and all the game animals on it. If the king liked to hunt, he didn't want anyone else taking "his" game. Suppose a peasant farmer went out and killed a rabbit or deer to feed his family. He could be tried for poaching and thrown in jail, if he didn't first get permission from the king to hunt. By law, in Tennessee, the game animals belong equally to all the citizens of the state. Once a year, the agency proposes open seasons for those game animals that can be hunted without harming the population of the species. When a hunter takes an animal by legal means, during open season, he can then assume ownership of that animal. When a poacher takes game illegally, he is stealing from all the citizens of the state of Tennessee. During the time when this area was first settled, wild game fed the folks who lived here. In many cases, it was the only meat they had unless they were lucky enough to have an extra beef, hog, or chicken on the farm. Even until the middle of the twentieth century, game probably appeared on many a table fairly often. As I mentioned in Chapter Six, that's just not necessary any longer.

Most poaching is done nowadays by thieves. They are usually engaged in other illegal activities such as theft, burglary, or drugs. Some may poach just for the thrill of it, but others are simply too lazy to make an honest living. One of our big headaches even up until the time I retired was spotlighting, or poaching at night. Mostly, this was done in remote areas of the county because the poachers didn't want to attract any attention to themselves. Attention meant increased chances of being caught. The prime area that I covered was in and around the Cherokee National Forest. The Cherokee National Forest is also a state wildlife management area, and this meant that even the possession of a firearm is illegal except during legal hunting seasons. Most of our spotlighting in those days took place just outside the national forest on privately owned land. For a long time, there were not many houses along much of Highway 107 in Houston Valley near the Greene-Cocke County line. We would occasionally get calls about spotlighting if the shooting did get too close to some of the houses, but mostly, we just knew that this was an area we needed to watch closely. Sometimes we contacted officers from near-by counties and set up details to work a certain area for several nights in a row. Then we might move to another county and work there for a few nights. These details were usually set up for Friday and Saturday nights because these were the nights when more poachers were out for a bit of "hunting." After a visit to one or more of the local "joints" and after the consumption of a few cold, adult beverages, these guys just couldn't wait to go out and "kill sumpthin."

Because of several complaints, Officer George and I had set up a detail with the Cocke County officers to work near the county line in Houston Valley. By this time, the state law had changed to make it illegal to shine a spotlight with the apparent attempt to locate game. You didn't have to be in possession of a firearm. This made our job a little easier, but these details were still not very productive. I think we had worked a couple of nights without any success, just long hours listening to the deer and other animals as they looked for a good meal. Then, I think it was on a Saturday night (maybe early Sunday morning), we were set up with a "catch truck" hidden on each end of several long pastures and another truck hidden in the woods to watch for the poachers. Officer George and I were on the Greene County end and the Cocke County officers had their end covered. Sometime around midnight, a vehicle came from Cocke County toward Greene County at a high rate of speed. All of a sudden, it slowed to a near stop and then proceeded on at maybe two or three miles per hour. Our watch-truck radioed Officer George and me, "Okay. We've got one. He's burning up this field right in front of me. Now he's shining the next field and the one across the road, too." Because Officer George and I were out of sight, we eased to our catch position without any lights on the truck and set up for the stop. The shiners were coming toward us so that meant we had to be ready to stop them as safely as possible without letting them get away. Escape was just not going to happen. We had spent too many long hours hiding in the woods to let them get away. The Cocke County boys, without any lights on, moved in behind the vehicle to prevent them from turning around. We now had the poachers between us. When we were satisfied that escape was not possible, the dark night lit up with blue lights. Just as the Cocke County boys pulled up behind the offending vehicle, I went to the driver's side and Officer George went to the passenger's side. My big Maglite beam hit the driver in the face as he reached down beside his seat in the apparent attempt to retrieve a weapon. I quickly got his attention and advised him very clearly that he should not make any further moves, not even to breathe. The racking of Officer George's Remington 870 shotgun got the other two occupants attention. All three were instructed to slowly show both hands with the warning that they had better be empty with the fingers spread. They later said that those were the biggest gun barrels they had ever seen. If they weren't sober when we stopped him, they were then. After getting the three men out of the vehicle, a quick check of the roadside located a Q-beam spotlight and a Remington 700 BDL, .270 caliber rifle with a scope. The vehicle they were driving was a 1970's Buick with leather seats and electric windows. It had a 454 cubic inch engine with two 4-barrel carburetors. All four tires were new, but all four were different brands. There were two vehicle identification numbers that we could find on the frame. One was registered to someone out of state and the other was registered to a car lot in still a different state. The license plate was registered to a car lot in Cocke County. We never did find the real owner of this "get away" Buick, and the state finally ended up selling it at public auction. Officer George and I wanted to keep it for undercover work, but we couldn't do that back then.

An inventory of the vehicle turned up several full and plenty of empty beer cans plus a couple of bloody hunting knives. This was in addition to the rifle and spotlight we found in the ditch. The back bumper was covered with what appeared to be dried blood with hair in it. The trunk also contained lots of blood and hair. I took samples of each from both the bumper and the trunk for analysis. The rifle, spotlight, and vehicle were seized as evidence, and the suspects were transported to the Greene County jail for processing. After all the necessary information was obtained from the three men and after they were given receipts for their equipment, they were left to post bond and await trial.

As the official agency "chemist" for this area, it was my duty to analyze the blood and hair samples for trial. At that time we had an immuno-diffusion process for identifying blood. The samples from both the vehicle's bumper and trunk tested positive for blood and also tested positive for deer blood. A trip to Walter State Community College's law enforcement lab allowed me to identify the hair samples as deer hair. Without question, a deer had been in the trunk of the Buick. This gave us all the evidence we needed to seize the vehicle under Tennessee's contraband laws. The defendants would not get it back. Since I was recognized by the court as an expert witness for both hair and blood identification, we had a good, strong case against these three men.

On the day for the trial, all the officers with all the evidence were on hand in the courtroom. I think the defendants knew that the verdict was never really in doubt. When the judge asked, "How do you plead?" they replied, "Guilty, Your Honor." The judge asked us for a summary of the case before he sentenced the defendants. After our short testimony the verdict was handed down. Guilty on all charges. The sentence for each man was the same, a maximum fine plus court costs, thirty days in jail, and confiscation of all equipment. This case was one of the first cases in Tennessee in which the defendants received jail time for wildlife violations.

One of the defendants was heard muttering to his buddies as they were escorted to jail, "I guess we shoulda been satisfied with the deer we had and not went back for another one."

13

Trout That Caught Themselves

*Go thou to the sea, and cast an hook, and take up the fish
that first cometh up.* — Matthew 17:27

After I began my career as a game warden/wildlife officer in Greene County, it didn't take me long to figure out that trout fishing is a very important activity for the local citizens. The Cherokee National Forest is blessed with many miles of mountain streams and creeks that have wild populations of rainbow, brown, and native brook trout. The little "brookie" is the only trout species native to the Southern Appalachian Mountains. It is found at higher elevations and usually requires a long, uphill hike to reach it. Some of the lower streams hold wild rainbows, while the middle elevation creeks will have some brown trout in them. Many fly fishermen enjoy hiking the trails leading up to these wild fish. To them, nothing is more satisfying than catching and releasing a few trout that have never felt a hook before.

However, not everyone is able to make the sometimes strenuous hikes up the mountain trails. Other folks would rather fish with bait or small spinning lures. For them, the agency has a trout stocking program. Each year, in the late winter and early fall, catchable size trout (9 to 14 inches) are released into lower creeks and streams in places with easy access. The fish for this area usually come from the Erwin rearing station mentioned in Chapter 9. Fingerlings are trucked to Erwin and reared in raceways and ponds until they are big enough to release. They are then loaded into tanks equipped with oxygen diffusers to keep them alive for transportation to the streams that are to be stocked that day. The fish can be kept in good shape for several hours in these special tanks while the truck is in route to its destination. We would usually meet the truck and assist in getting the trout safely to the creek. This meant carrying big dip nets full of fish and running as fast as we could without spilling the fish. If we lost any trout, we could count on some good natured kidding from the rearing station guys and some advice on how to keep such "accidents" from happening again. Fortunately, we learned really quickly not to lose any trout. They were important to the fishermen!

The streams that are normally stocked in Greene County are Horse Creek, Camp Creek, and Paint Creek in the Cherokee National Forest. For several years, two young men from the local high school took it upon themselves to help us stock Paint Creek. They soon learned how to handle the fish, how to regulate the oxygen, and how to do all the other things necessary to get the trout into the creek. These guys surely made things easier for us. We mostly just rode in the truck while they did all the work. Since they were supposed to be in school, we worried about their getting into trouble with their teachers, but they assured us that each teacher gave them permission to be absent for a short time if they made up any missed work. I guess both boys did okay because they graduated on time and got good jobs afterwards. They would come back to fish the creek after school, but they never tried to put fish anywhere that wasn't equally accessible for everyone. They were just good sportsmen who enjoyed helping us. Many times, we had a long parade of folks following the truck just to see where we stocked the trout. That was okay, but I never could figure out what good it did to watch us. The fish usually didn't bite much for a while after they were in the streams, and by that time, they had pretty much scattered up and down the creek.

Once the stocking was complete, we would say good-by to the Erwin folks and begin patrolling the streams to check licenses and to count fish. This was generally a pretty routine activity because folks wouldn't catch over their limit if they knew the game warden was near-by. Some might take their limit home and then come back for more, but we usually could remember the ones we had previously checked. I was patrolling Camp Creek late one afternoon and was just about ready to call it quits and go home. Then I saw a young man standing next to the creek as it meandered through a pasture. He was just standing there doing nothing but looking around. "Now that's odd," I thought. My natural officer curiosity told me to go check him out so I parked the truck and walked over to him. "Howdy, son. What are you doing out here?"

"Oh, nothing."

"Nothing?" I asked. "You're not fishing?"

"No, Sir. I don't fish." Well, I guess he was just communing with nature. Some folks like to do that. Then I noticed a tree limb stuck into the creek bank. It looked out of place so I went to investigate (Again, officer curiosity). There, looped over the limb, was a fish stringer with about eight or ten nice rainbow trout on it.

"Are these your fish?" I asked.

"No, Sir. Never seen them before." As I looked around for more evidence, I saw something long and blue on the creek bottom a short distance away. My water-proof Browning boots served me well this time as I retrieved a fishing rod complete with spinning reel, line, and hook from the creek.

"Is this your rod?" I asked.

"No, Sir. Never seen it before."

"Son, you're the only one around. These fish are alive and well so they haven't been here too long. The rod was in the creek right where you were standing. Think hard. Are you sure you don't know how they got here?"

Again, he replied, "No, Sir. I don't have any idea." Well, you have probably guessed by now that he saw me before I saw him. He had time to throw his rod into the creek, but he didn't have time to make his get-away. I guess he decided that just standing there looking kind of dumb wouldn't attract as much attention as running away. I did not see him with the pole in his hand so I really couldn't swear in court that I saw him fishing. Since I always wanted a strong case when I went to court, and since he was a juvenile, I wrote down all his pertinent information and confiscated the trout and rod and reel. I advised the young man to talk to his parents and, if he thought of anything he wanted to tell me or if he wanted to claim the rod and reel, to give me a call. I did not hear anything more from him, but I really didn't expect to get a confession. I did know where he went to school, however. Because we regularly presented programs to most of the schools, I knew most of the teachers and principals. A visit to this young man's gym teacher and a couple of his other teachers assured that the story of the trout that hooked themselves would be told all over the school. The kidding that this boy endured from his friends and teachers over the next couple of weeks probably did more good than a trip to court. I think I donated the trout to the county jail or to some "worthy recipient." I still have the rod and reel, if the young man wants to claim it.

14

Ma'am, I'm Not That TV Fisherman

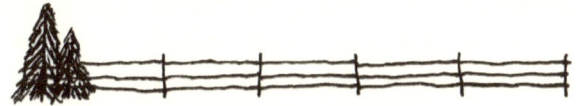

And He said unto them,
"Cast the net on the right side of the ship,
and ye shall find [some fish]. — John 21:6

L et's continue with another short fish tale. Not long after the agency came into being in the mid 1970's, an emphasis began to be placed on "information and education." Instead of keeping to themselves, officers were encouraged to be more available to the sportsmen and general public. We were told to stop in at the country stores, buy a soda, and visit with the folks awhile. We were to be on hand if a civic club, school, or a church group wanted us to present a fish or wildlife related program to them. The agency has a really good film library with films (now videos) on everything from constructing a farm pond to identifying snakes. Many of the films were geared toward younger audiences and became very popular with elementary schools and young church groups. Soon, in addition to law enforcement duties, we were kept busy giving talks and showing films all over the county. I always liked to get requests for programs from civic clubs because that usually meant a good meal went along with the program. The agency also began to print posters and fliers to give to people. We would put up the posters in the courthouse, stores, and other places where we thought they might be seen by a lot of folks, and we would leave a supply of fliers or handouts to go with them.

Local newspapers are also a good way to get information to the sportsmen and we were encouraged to use them. Some officers wrote regular columns for their newspapers. My newspaper was always very helpful to me, even though I didn't write a column for them. They already had good outdoor writers, but they would print anything that I wanted and were very cooperative in informing folks about important wildlife news.

Another thing that the agency did was to improve the hunting and fishing guides so that they provided much more information than just listing the seasons. Fish and wildlife identification guides, "how to" guides for farmers, lake and wildlife management area maps, and many other publications would soon be available to everyone. The more folks got to know us, the more they realized that we weren't just out there to write them a citation. Also, the more informed the sportsmen became, the fewer "mistake" violations occurred. We could concentrate more on the real bad guys who were breaking the game laws on purpose. This emphasis on information and education proved to be one of the best things that the new agency started doing.

Now, back to my fish tale. Probably the best way to get information to as many people as possible is through radio and television. Wildlife officers were encouraged to approach our local radio and television stations about allowing us to have a short spot for a wildlife program. Since there were no television stations in Greene County at that time, I went to Radio Greeneville, Inc. They had both AM and FM stations serving the Greene County area. The son and grandson of the owner were and still are avid sportsmen so it didn't take too long to get permission for a weekly radio program that we called "The Outdoor Report with Bill Nance." This title would cause a bit of confusion for one listener a few years down the road. More about that later. I first started recording the program on reel tape and then it would be played over the air at a certain time during the week. Now, of course, I just record it on a computer and it does the rest. Sometimes, I would present the program live, if we had something important to tell the folks or if the radio station just wanted to do it a little differently every once in a while.

If you watch fishing shows on television or live in Tennessee, you are probably familiar with a television fishing program hosted by a professional fisherman with a name very similar to mine. He always wears a Tennessee Vols cap and is quite popular in this state. He must be a good fisherman because a lot of people watch his programs. I've never met him, but maybe I will someday so I can tell him this tale. I was doing a live program at the radio station one day when a lady called in during the broadcast. The receptionist at the station talked to her while I was on the air, but, apparently, was not able to satisfactorily answer her questions.

When my program was over, the receptionist handed me the phone and said, "Here! You talk to her!"

"This is Bill Nance. May I help you?"

She replied, "I know who you are. I want you to tell me where to go fishing." I told her that I would be glad to give her the information that I had from the latest fishing reports. "No! I want you to tell me where you go fishing. I watch you on television and you always catch a lot of fish. I want to go fish where you go."

As politely as I could without giggling too much, I informed her, "Ma'am, I'm not that television fisherman."

"Oh yes you are. I watch you every week. You're just trying to keep your fishing spots a secret. Now you tell me where I can catch some fish." Again, I tried to tell her that I'm not the guy she watched on television, but I didn't have much luck. She finally hung up the phone, thoroughly convinced that I just didn't want her to catch any fish and that I was the meanest television fisherman she had ever encountered.

After I retired, Radio Greeneville asked me to keep presenting my "Outdoor Report." Most Greene County listeners knew me since I had been on the air for almost thirty years and they looked forward to the program. Now, some fourteen years later, "The Outdoor Report with Bill Nance" is the longest running regularly scheduled radio program in Greene County and has approximately 28,000 listeners each week.

15

Antelope Stew and "Tenderloin"Supper

Thou shalt not eat any abominable thing.
These are the beasts which ye shall eat: the ox,
the sheep, the goat, the deer, ... the antelope ...
— Deuteronomy 14:3-5

In order to do my job properly, I felt strongly, from the time I went to work, that I had to develop a good working relationship with the other officers in my area. Without neglecting my own work, I tried very hard to keep that good relationship in place throughout my entire career. Many of the officers from other departments were avid hunters and fishermen. Most were raised on farms and enjoyed being outdoors when they weren't working. They wanted to see the game laws enforced and were always willing to pass along any information they might have learned from their investigations, if they thought it would help me to solve a wildlife case. They also saw the need to work together to protect both the public and our natural resources. Other departments were always quick to loan me special equipment if I needed something they had, and most officers were more than willing to give me advice on cases that were similar to some they had worked. Remember, most law breakers do not specialize in just one crime. If they violate game laws, they are likely to violate other laws too. I dealt with some of the same folks that the police department and sheriff's department encountered in their work. Any assistance that I received from their officers was always greatly appreciated. With their help, we made some really good wildlife cases over the years.

After I had been working for several years, I got the idea that it would be nice if I could do something for my fellow lawmen to show my appreciation for all their help. The opportunity to do just that arose when one of my volunteer hunter education instructors invited me to join him and a couple of his friends on an antelope hunt out west. These volunteer instructors were vital to making our hunter education program a success, and I was lucky enough to have some of the best of the sportsmen and teachers from the very beginning of the program. G.J. was one of the most reliable and knowledgeable instructors that we ever had. He and some of his friends had gone to Wyoming a few times to hunt antelope on a thirty thousand acre ranch in the eastern part of the state. They got to know the folks who worked the ranch and earned their trust to the extent that they could go pretty much anywhere they wanted to hunt. We could camp on the ranch and hunt where we pleased because the ranchers knew we would be careful of the cattle and ranch property. When G.J. asked me if I wanted to go with them, he didn't have to ask again. The hunt would be in early October so I would be back by the time the deer season opened here. I had enough vacation time built up so that it was not too hard to get off from work for a few days. Before we left for Wyoming, I discussed the up-coming hunt with several of the Greeneville police officers and asked for hunting tips and such from them. We even borrowed a camper from one of the auxiliary officers. Several of them sent us off with their wishes for a good hunt and a request for a pot of antelope stew if we were successful. Here was my chance to do something to show my appreciation to the other officers. All I had to do was to take an antelope on the hunt and I could fix them a good supper one night after I got back.

When we got to the ranch, we checked in with the ranchers, set up camp, and scouted around for a while. We saw several herds of nice antelope and picked out some good areas to hunt. Over the next few days, when we weren't helping the ranchers work cattle (we tried to earn our welcome), most of us were able to harvest a couple of antelope. I took a nice buck with decent sized horns and a younger one that would be nice and tender for our antelope supper. It was a great hunt with great companions on a ranch with some really nice folks for hosts. Once back in Greeneville, the meat went to the local packing house for processing while we began the mandatory post hunt storytelling. When I had my antelope all stored in the freezer, I contacted Lieutenant K and his 3-11 shift about fixing supper for them one night. They were unanimous. "Oh, yes! That would be great." We agreed on a date and I got busy preparing the meal.

Now I do a lot of cooking and it was no problem to fix a big pot of antelope stew, cornbread, salad, and all the trimmings. To go along with the stew, I decided to fix the guys a special treat and asked the lieutenant if it would be okay to do that. "By all means," he replied. "That sure sounds good to me." A quick trip back to the local packing house got me a big sack of very fresh "mountain oysters."

Authors Note: If you don't know what "mountain oysters" are, google the term for a definition and some tasty recipes.

After a little work with a sharp fileting knife and some hot grease, I had a big platter of what looked like pork tenderloin to go with the antelope stew and cornbread. When everything was ready in the kitchen at the police department, I told the guys to "come and get it." The lieutenant said he would stay on patrol while the others ate. That was surely thoughtful of him, but, you remember, he knew about my "special treat" I told the officers that I wasn't sure everyone would like the antelope stew so I fried some (chuckle) "tenderloin" just in case. Like most lawmen, these guys didn't have to be told twice that supper was ready. They quickly devoured most of the stew, cornbread, and "tenderloin". "Hey, save some for the lieutenant. He wants to eat, too."

About that time, Lieutenant K walked through the door, and his troops greeted him with, "Better hurry. It sure is good but it's almost gone." Some of the guys were a little suspicious of the "tenderloin", but it was so good that they just ate it and didn't say much about it. Then one of the officers asked the lieutenant if he thought it was really tenderloin.

"It's good but I don't know for sure. Let me try another piece. Yep, I think I know what it is. Just one more and I'll be positive." After another helping had disappeared, the Lieutenant said, "I've got it! Those are mountain oysters!"

The last I saw of two of the officers, they were in fifth gear, headed out the door. A couple of other guys had almost torn the door off the soda machine and the rest were just sitting there looking about as green as a game warden's truck. Lieutenant K and I had a good time enjoying the show and finishing up the rest of the stew and "tenderloin." Even if I did cook it, I thought we had a pretty good meal. I never really quite understood why the other two shifts didn't say anything about my fixing supper for them. Oh, well. I guess they just didn't like antelope stew or something. It is a little strange that, after all these years, some of those guys still won't eat anything I cook. Maybe if I tried bear stew next time??

16

Road Kill and Moonshine

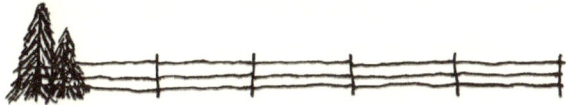

Wine is a mocker, strong drink is raging:
and whosoever is deceived thereby is not wise. — Proverbs 20:1

As I have mentioned earlier, one of the things that made my wildlife career so enjoyable was that each day and each patrol seemed to result in something different to do. No activity was ever the same. What started out as a routine assignment might end up being a very exciting day. We never knew when we would drive up on a violation in progress, or some lady would run out into the yard yelling that a bear had just run through her garden. These things happened more often than you might think. I could always count on a slow day ending up with something unusual happening. This sometimes meant plenty of overtime hours before we restored order and got everything back to normal. Other than arresting someone, I can think of only two activities that I never really enjoyed. One was the long, hot days in a boat on a lake with rough water, blazing sun, and no shade. The other, as I mentioned in Chapter 7, was picking up and disposing of road killed animals.

One day while I was on a "routine patrol" in the western part of Greene County, I got a radio call from the sheriff's department. They informed me that someone had run over a deer on the Asheville highway about ten miles out of town. The dispatcher told me to hurry and get over there as soon as I could because the newly deceased animal was a traffic hazard and needed to be removed at once.

"Well, why couldn't they just drag it off the road until I could find someone who might want it," I thought. "That way I won't have to bother with it."

"No," the dispatcher said. "You need to go take care of it." Oh boy, another sore back and ruined uniform. I made every excuse I could think of to delay this unpleasant job for as long as possible. I think I even stopped for a soda and a moon pie a couple of times. What the dispatcher couldn't tell me over the radio, was that the sheriff's department, highway patrol, Tennessee Bureau of Investigation, and the Alcoholic Beverage boys were going to raid a still and wanted to invite me to go with them. Of course they couldn't say anything over the radio because so many folks had police scanners. The still operator would be long gone when the "revenuers" arrived.

For those of you who aren't mountain folk; moonshining, or the making of illegal, untaxed whiskey, was not that unusual up and down the Appalachian Mountains. It became fairly common after the Revolutionary War when farmers in remote areas found that they could transport and sell "liquid corn" much easier and much faster than the grain itself. The profit was a little higher, too. The government frowned on such activity because the whiskey tax brought in a fair amount of money for the new country. Moonshining became a clandestine occupation that usually took place in remote, hidden hollows or other places where the smoke from the boiler fire couldn't be seen. The moonshiners also wanted to make it as hard as possible for the revenuers, or government agents, to find and get to their stills. Thus, the making of white lightening became a game for the "shine" makers. "Catch us if you can. We'll pay the fine and be back in business by tomorrow night." Many moonshiners were well known in their communities and some even achieved a degree of notoriety throughout America due to movies, songs, and, later, television.

Illegal stills were still common throughout Appalachia when I came to work in Greene County. I heard stories about those who made "likker" and where their stills were located. "Best not go poking around up that holler, Mr. Warden. The ol' man that lives up there might not like it too much." I always tried to let folks know that I was in their neighborhood and that I was only checking on game violations. I never had any trouble at all with moonshiners during my career.

.Well, enough of the history lesson. The high price of sugar, illegal drugs, and modern law enforcement techniques had reduced the number of moonshiners drastically by the time I had worked a few years, but there were a few folks that just couldn't break the habit of cookin' corn. The person targeted by the Greene County officers on the day they called me to go with them was just such a man. He had made "shine" all his life and his daddy had done the same thing. It was in their blood in more ways than one. After I had made all the excuses that I could, I finally arrived at the scene of the "road killed deer." Yep, I was too late to go on the raid, but I did see the results. The owner-operator was not at home and was not found near his stills. Maybe the local grapevine had worked and he was tipped off after all. The officers did confiscate four stills and several gallons of moonshine. The stills were all loaded on trucks for transportation to a secure location until they could be destroyed by court order. There were a couple of really good quality stills with stainless steel boilers and plumbing. I suppose these were for making the "good stuff." I remember another still that was made from an old truck radiator and was plumbed with galvanized pipe. Probably, the moonshine from this still was for folks that the operator didn't particularly like. He may not have had too many repeat customers for this product. Of the liquor that was confiscated, some of it was in the standard glass canning jars. Some more was in crock jugs of various sizes, and some in really well-made solid oak barrels that held about six or eight gallons of "shine." The moonshiner was probably going to sell this last batch as aged whiskey. Aged about as long as it took to sell it, that is. Although I have no use for the contents of the barrels, an empty one of them would have made a nice addition to my law enforcement memorabilia. If I hadn't delayed going to pick up the "road kill", I could have had a good souvenir. The next time, I listened to the dispatcher and was never late to assist another officer.

17

"Knock Him Out, John"

*To everything there is a season, and a time for every purpose
under the heavens: A time to weep and a time to laugh.*
— Ecclesiastes 3:1, 4a

Law enforcement is not a career to pursue if a person is looking for
a lot of personal recognition and awards. You might try beauty
pageants or politics if that's important to you. Since law enforcement
is a public service occupation, I believe that one cannot do a good
job serving the public if he continually puts himself first. Many law
enforcement agencies have the motto, "To Protect and Serve." If an
officer concentrates on protecting and serving the people for whom
he works, and does his job well, some recognition will come. Some
local groups and even a few national organizations honor officers
for a job well done, but most recognition will probably come in the
form of a promotion to a higher rank within the department. In my
case, a promotion was not likely unless I left the law enforcement

division. Since I didn't want to do that, I retired after thirty years as a wildlife officer.

However, my agency does recognize an "Officer of the Year" and, in 1976, I was fortunate enough to be selected as Region 4 Officer of the Year and then state-wide Officer of the Year. As a result of this honor, I was allowed to attend the Southeastern Association convention in Jackson, Mississippi, to receive my award. Most of these conventions are not too exciting, but I looked forward to going just for the experience. We had the obligatory workshops to attend for a couple of days, and then everything closed with a big banquet on the last night. I must say that Mississippi did feed us well with all the fried catfish, hush puppies, and trimmings we could eat. After the meal and after the awards were presented to all the southeastern folks, it was time for the main speaker.

Mr. Jerry Clower, dressed in a yellow tuxedo and yellow cowboy boots, stepped to the microphone. I knew immediately that we were in for a real treat and he didn't disappoint us. Mr. Clower came early, before the banquet, and spent some time talking to as many officers as he could. I got to meet him and we joked about coon hunters and some of the problems they occasionally cause us. During his talk, he told some of the coon hunting tales and Marcel Ledbetter stories that we all pretty well knew by memory. He also talked about his strong Christian faith and how that could help officers to deal with the problems and tragedies we sometimes face. Mr. Clower certainly knew how to relate to his audience and we thoroughly enjoyed the evening.

Now, county fairs are pretty big events in many of the rural counties in the South. Tennessee is no exception. Greene County has its fair each year in August, and a few years after the Mississippi convention, they announced that Jerry Clower would headline the program one night. Well, I couldn't miss the opportunity to go hear Mr. Clower again. His stories and jokes never get old for some of us. I went early so I could be up close to the front and ended up helping with security at one end of the stage. Sure enough, here came Mr. Clower in his yellow tuxedo and yellow cowboy boots for the first of two shows. Anyone who wears yellow cowboy boots is okay in my book (I'm originally from Texas). He began his stories and they were about the same as we heard in Mississippi but they were still entertaining and funny. At one point he stopped and said that he didn't recognize people in the audience unless they were from Route 4, Liberty, Mississippi, or unless they played football for Mississippi State University. There just happened to be a man in the audience who met both requirements so Mr. Clower had him stand up. A few more coon hunting tales and talks about his childhood days ended the first show. Of course I planned to stay for the second one too. There was no thought of leaving so I just stayed around the end of the stage while Mr. Clower rested and relaxed in a makeshift dressing room backstage. After a couple of minutes, someone came up to me and said, "Mr. Clower wants to see you backstage." I didn't know that he was even aware of my presence, but it sure didn't take me long to make my way to the dressing room. As I reached the door, he waved me in and then said, "I just got to have me a chew of that Beechnut that you have in your pocket before the next show." I quickly handed him my pack of Beechnut chewing tobacco (I've long since quit the habit) and we sat down on some coke crates that were in the room to enjoy a "chaw." You older folks will remember those wooden crates that held two dozen soft drink bottles. Well, they could be used for lots of things besides holding bottles. I reminded Mr. Clower about the Mississippi convention, and we discussed things that had happened since then. He was very friendly and we talked just like a couple of old neighbors sitting on the front porch. I think that's just the way a lot of southern folks are. After swapping a few funny hunting tales and a few life experiences, the fair people had to come get us when it was time for the next show. I took my place at one end of the stage and Mr. Clower began his stories. Whenever he told a hunting tale he would look over at me and say, "Mr. Game Warden, that happened out of your jurisdiction." or "Mr. Game Warden, pretend you didn't hear that." To me, that was better than being recognized for attending Mississippi State or for being from Liberty, Mississippi.

Mr. Jerry Clower was very much a southern gentleman who lived his Christian faith and loved to entertain folks. I was privileged to meet him and to be able to spend a little time swapping tales with him.

18

Come In. Mr. Warden

Be not forgetful to entertain strangers: for thereby some have entertained angels unawares. — Hebrews 13:2

Or maybe some have entertained game wardens unawares. When I first came to work in Greene County, there were only two deer taken on hunts in the county outside of the wildlife management area. Due to the agency's restocking program, the deer population began to increase rapidly in all areas of the county. We discovered that deer could live and thrive on farmland and even near towns and other populated areas. Soon, we were able to open more and more territory to hunting. First, the southern half of the county was opened and then, a short time later, the northern half of the county was ready for hunting. I think the rapid increase in deer population was, for the most part, due to the protection they received from the folks who were glad to see them around and were quick to report poaching activities.

One year when the deer season was still a big thing, I got a call about someone shooting a deer out of a vehicle on a public road. This was in the northern part of Greene County near Baileyton. The deer season hadn't been open very long in that area and folks were still pretty protective of them. It took me thirty minutes or so to get to the location that I had been given, and, by the time I got there, the violators were long gone. However, I was able to find a couple of witnesses and to talk to them. They gave me a very good description of the shooters and their vehicle. Most of the time we got descriptions like, "It was either a small car or a big truck and it was either blue, red, or white." These witnesses knew what they had seen and told me that the shooters were two young boys, possibly juveniles. They were sure about the make, model, and color of the truck, and even gave me a partial license plate number. I pulled my truck off the road and into a safe place where I could watch the area in case the violators came back. Since all license plates sold in any given county have a specific pattern to the combination of numbers and letters, I wrote down a few possible plate numbers that could have been issued in Greene County. After running a registration check on a few of these through the National Crime Information Center (N.C.I.C.), I got a hit on one that was registered to a truck matching the description of the suspect vehicle. The address of the owner was only a few miles up the road from my location. How about that. "This must be my lucky day," I thought. What more could an officer ask for than a good description, a license plate hit, and an address not far away. All I would need to do was to go arrest the violators.

As you will see, things are never as easy as we would like for them to be. For my safety, I radioed the sheriff's department to advise them of my destination and to alert them that I would be conducting an active investigation at that address. I had no trouble finding the right road, but it turned out to be a one lane gravel "driveway" that led toward the foot of Fodderstack Mountain in a very remote part of the county. The address I was looking for was the last trailer on the road right at the base of the mountain. Just a couple of steps out the back door would require one to begin climbing a steep slope. The truck that I was looking for was not there, but another one was parked in the front yard. Somebody must be home so I radioed the Sheriff's department again to tell them that I had arrived at my destination and would be out of my vehicle. When I got out of my truck, I saw a fresh deer hide and some deer feet in the back of the truck in the yard. There were also several freshly gnawed bones scattered around the yard. The dogs must have had an early lunch. Standing to one side of the door, I knocked and heard a voice inside say, "Come in, Mr. Warden." A big red flag went up at this point. I eased the door open and, presenting as small a target as possible, carefully stepped inside. The first thing I saw was a rifle leaning against the door frame. A very quick look around the trailer showed me that there were two adults in the kitchen area. One was male and the other was female. Both were holding large butcher knives. Since the two were fifteen feet or so away, the rifle seemed to be the first priority. I picked it up, unloaded it and put the cartridges into my pocket for safe-keeping. Meanwhile, the man and woman went back to doing what they were doing when I drove up. They were cutting up large pieces of red meat and wrapping them for the freezer. I could see that the meat was dark red and had no fat on it. It certainly wasn't beef or pork. "Howdy folks. Mind telling me what you are doing."

"Oh, we're just cutting up a deer our son brought home this morning." was their reply.

"Okay. Then I guess I need to see the kill tag." They were unable to produce a valid kill tag for the alleged deer, and they also couldn't give me a believable explanation for where they got the deer. At this point I advised them that they were under arrest and told them to put down the knives. They complied and, after securing the rifle, I took them outside where things were safer and then radioed for back-up from the sheriff's department. I advised the two suspects of their rights and began questioning the woman about the two juveniles. When I asked who they were, she said that one of the juveniles was her son and the other was his friend. They were out hunting and she didn't know when they would be back. She also informed me that the son had brought the deer home earlier that morning and told them to butcher it while he went back to hunt for another one. Both the man and woman were very cooperative and told me anything I wanted to know.

After about a half an hour my back up arrived and we began the process of securing the evidence and inventorying it. I confiscated all the meat, the knives and the rifle. I wrote the man and woman the appropriate citations and told them that I needed to see their son and his friend as soon as possible. After saving a couple of packages of meat for evidence, the rest went to feed the prisoners in the county jail. It took a few trips back to the trailer to locate the son, but I finally caught him at home. He was not nearly as cooperative as his parents and wouldn't tell me much of anything about the case. However, I felt that I had enough evidence to cite him to juvenile court and wrote out the necessary paperwork without further questioning. I later found his friend at school and cited him to court also. The principal of the high school told me that the son rarely came to school and, when he did, he spent most of the time in detention hall. He was failing most subjects and was far from a model student.

As I mentioned previously, I was the area lab chemist for the agency, so it was no problem to run a blood identification check on the confiscated meat. I extracted some blood from the meat and ran the standard diffusion test on it. There was no question about it; the blood was deer blood. So now I had them in possession of deer meat and a rifle, but no hunting license or kill tag. Pretty strong evidence to take to court.

When we got to court, the folks on trial became much less cooperative than they were when I first questioned them. They had all kinds of excuses for why they had an illegally taken deer and why their son was involved in poaching instead of going to school. I just let them have their say and then presented my case to the judge in a professional manner. You can probably figure out whom the judge believed. The other juvenile had already posted a cash bond and forfeited it so he wasn't involved in the trial. I don't think he wanted anything more to do with his buddy after that. Smart kid!

From what I learned about this family, this was not the first deer they had poached and I'm sure it wasn't the last. The son has been an adult for some time now and he has been in trouble with the law most of his life. I guess if they learned anything from this case, it was, if you're going to poach deer, be careful when you say, "Come in, Mr. Warden."

19

Texas Game Warden for a Night

Man goeth forth unto his work and to his labor until the evening.
— Psalm 104:23

In chapter one I discussed what it was like growing up in Southeast Texas on the Gulf Coast. I was pretty much able to do as I pleased after I got a little older. Sure, I had chores that I was expected to get done on time, but, as long as I did them, I was free to enjoy growing up in a rural area. When I was a kid, young people just didn't disobey the adults in their lives, so I was always careful to get my work done before going to play. The last thing on earth that I wanted was to have my granddad upset with me. Especially after I got a little older, playing usually meant hunting or fishing either on the farm or on some relative's land. We also had a fish camp on Trinity Bay where we could catch plenty of redfish, flounder, and speckled trout. There was always an abundant supply of small game available, but no big game. Squirrels, rabbits, quail, doves, coons, and all kinds of waterfowl were everywhere. My buddy and I made good use of my uncle's duck blind to hunt mallards, teal, pintail, geese, brant, and puldoo (coots to you non Cajuns). We just didn't have any deer, turkey, bear, or hogs. One had to go to West Texas to hunt those. Alligators were also almost unheard of, but more about those guys later.

By the time I became a game warden in Tennessee, my grandparents had passed away and my mother was developing some major health problems. I had also lost touch with most of my high school friends over the years. Some had moved away and others had their own families and friends. The small town had really grown and there wasn't much farmland left. All my old hunting places now had houses on them. My mother was about the only one left to visit in my hometown, but I tried to make the thousand mile trip as often as possible to see her. She soon became confined to her house and, later, to a bed for several years. When I went for a visit, I would spend the days just talking to her or running errands for her. She had to have a nurse with her most of the time so I usually got a motel room close by. Since I didn't know too many people around town and didn't know the area very well, I usually spent most nights watching the Houston Astros on television. Although my mother kept me busy during the day, enjoying a good seafood supper was about all I had to do after she got settled for the night.

On one trip during the summer, I decided to give the local wildlife officer a call. I thought it would be fun to compare experiences and to see what his job was like. The local police department gave me his number and I was able to get in touch with him without much trouble. After talking awhile on the phone, I soon discovered that we had many similar problems, and pretty much did things the same way. He did tell me that they now had an abundance of deer and turkeys (just like back home in Tennessee). He also mentioned that they were overrun with alligators, but more about those guys later. After some more tale-swapping, he mentioned that he would be working the next night and asked if I would like to ride with him. Would I? That sounded like a lot more fun than watching the Astros. He said he would pick me up at my motel at eight o'clock and we would go out on patrol for his shift. I didn't have a uniform with me, but I did have a t-shirt with a printed badge on the front and the word "POLICE" in big letters across the back. Oh well, I guess that would have to do. Sure enough, at eight o'clock the next night, here came a big grey truck with "Texas Parks and Wildlife" on the door. We introduced ourselves and he said, "Let's roll."

"Wait a minute. I need to ask you something first. What about my weapon?"

He replied, "If you aren't wearing it, you're not riding with me."

With a "Police" t-shirt, a Glock .40 cal. pistol, and blue jeans as my uniform, we took off. It was a typical hot, steamy Texas summer night; just right for a night of fishing. We drove around to some good fishing holes on the bayous and on some creeks. We checked a few fishermen but didn't run into anything out of the ordinary. "Let's go see what's happening over on the ship channel," he decided. Up until now, no one had questioned my "uniform" or my authority to check Texas fishing licenses. So far, so good. The Houston Ship Channel was where we were headed now. It extends from Galveston Bay up to the Port of Houston, and runs close to where I grew up. Here, we found quite a few fishermen and crabbers. Many were Hispanic since that part of Texas has always had a large population of Latin Americans. We saw a few nice stringers of fish, mostly croakers and sand trout. The crabs seemed to be biting that night, too. Texas bay crabs are mighty tasty and sure do make good gumbo. We checked many licenses, but didn't run into any violators. Still, no one questioned me or even seemed to notice that I was dressed a little different from my partner. At one time, we were joined by some Harris County deputies and we all spent several hours driving up and down the channel. All night, I had noticed some large signs warning people to stay out of the water because the undertow was dangerous. They were printed in both English and Spanish, but nobody seemed to pay much attention to them. A lot of the fishermen we saw were out in the water at least chest deep. I asked my Texas partner about the signs and he said that the big ships going to and from the Port of Houston caused the undertow. There are some very large tankers and freighters that use the channel, and the backwash from their huge propellers creates a strong current that will pull a person right out into the channel. Sadly, he said that they routinely have to search for people who have drowned while fishing. Just like in Tennessee, some folks don't seem to pay much attention to warning signs or other important information even when it can save their lives. It's the same reasoning that is used to justify not wearing a life jacket or a seat belt, I guess.

From the Houston Ship Channel, we drove a few miles northeast to Lake Houston. This is a twelve thousand-acre lake (compared to Douglas Lake in East Tennessee with 28,500 acres) that didn't exist when I lived in Harris County. Now, it is the second main water source for the city of Houston and is a favorite recreational lake and wilderness area. Once again, we fell into the routine of checking fishing licenses without finding a single violation. I guess that was probably for the better. A Texas judge might have wanted to know what I was doing lawing people in his state, anyway. If I remember correctly, out of all the fishermen we checked that night, only one citation was written, and that was one which a deputy wrote for possessing open beer or something.

The rest of the shift was spent sightseeing at some of the places I used to go as a teenager. We mostly drove and talked about our jobs. Apparently, Texas had undertaken restocking programs for deer and turkey similar to the Tennessee programs. Texas Parks and Wildlife seemed to be just as successful as my agency because my partner said that they now had huntable populations of both animals everywhere in the state. They were even getting complaints about turkeys on carports and deer eating gardens. That surely sounded familiar. All in all, I think most southern wildlife officers face similar problems and do things pretty much the same way. By now, it was getting late (or early morning) and the shift was about over. I thought I had better get a little sleep before time to go check on my mother anyway. All night long, I kept noticing a rather large dent in the hood of the big grey truck in which we were riding. I thought now would be a good time to ask my partner how it got there. "Oh, that," he said casually. "That was made by a twelve foot gator I had to rassle out of a pond right behind your old house. With that, we arrived back at the motel. I thanked my Texas partner for the great experience of being a Texas game warden for a night. We said our good-byes, and wished each other continued safety in our work.

The next morning, I purposely forgot to mention anything to my mother about the big gator that was right behind her house. She didn't need to have anything like that to worry about. The rest of my visit passed quickly and it was time to head home to Tennessee. Even though I thoroughly enjoyed this trip to Texas, had a good visit with my mother, and got to be a Texas game warden for a night, it was good to be on the road home. Every few miles along the way I remembered to thank the Good Lord for sending me to East Tennessee for my wildlife career instead of leaving me in Southeast Texas. You see, I could handle the bear and deer poachers, the coon hunters and the little old ladies who thought I was a famous television fisherman, but there's no way on earth that I had any desire to end up rasslin' big old gators out of ponds.

20

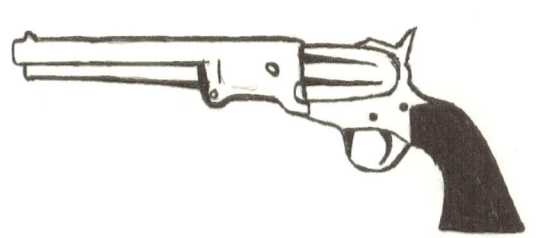

The Shootin' Iron That Didn't Swim

And the man of God said, Where fell it?
And he shewed him the place. And he cut down a stick,
and cast it in thither; and the iron did swim. — 2 Kings 6:6

About half way through my career, the agency began to place more and more emphasis on boating safety education and enforcement. The area lakes weren't just for fishing anymore. They were becoming very popular as recreational areas as well. Also, the number of boat owners was increasing at a faster rate than ever before. These new boats weren't small fishing boats; they were larger and faster boats and were used, many times, for both fishing and recreation. Water skiers could be pulled easily by the big engines that were now available. A few years later, jet skis entered the market and became an instant success. The popularity of bass tournaments attracted new and old fishermen alike. It wasn't unusual for these bass boats to be capable of running eighty miles per hour. The tournament fishermen just had to be able to beat their buddies to the best fishing spots. Pontoon boats were a good way for a family to spend a leisurely day on the water or for friends to enjoy some quiet fishing back in a cove. The area lakes soon became filled with people and boats, especially on the weekends and holidays. Slow moving john boats, fast bass boats, water skiers, wake jumping jet skis, and drifting pontoon boats all made for a lethal mix on the water. Add to this traffic jam, the hot sun, wave action and, for some, a drink or two or three; and things could become tragic in a hurry. Boating accidents resulting in serious injury and death became all too common on our lakes and rivers. To make matters worse, folks weren't wearing their personal flotation devices (life jackets) as they should, and many night fishermen refused to display the required lighting after dark. Many fatal accidents happened when a boater ran over a fisherman because the fishing boat was almost invisible at night.

Something had to be done to make the public more aware of the hazards on the water. The agency began a program of education aimed at boaters and also offered boating safety classes similar to the hunter education classes. A commitment was made to put more officers on patrol on the lakes and rivers and to have them on duty both day and night. The officers' presence and some citations mostly for improper life jackets and light violations began to get folks' attention. A $100 fine for not having the proper personal flotation devices on board or for not turning on lights at night would act as a pretty good reminder for the next outing. At first, this increase in lake work for the officers did not affect those of us who didn't have big lakes in our county. I continued to patrol the much cooler national forest in my air conditioned truck while the lake guys were sweltering in open boats with no shady spots out on the water. However, that all changed. Soon almost every officer was assigned to work the lakes and rivers on weekends and holidays, and, sometimes, several days during the week. So much for air conditioned trucks. At first, I was assigned to work most of the time with the Hawkins County officer on Cherokee Lake. Officer Geo had worked several years longer than I, and had been in Hawkins County for a number of years. He knew everybody and everybody knew him. He was well liked in and around his area. During all the time I spent working with

Officer Geo, I don't believe I ever heard anyone say anything bad about him. He got along well with the courts, sportsmen, boat dock operators, and just about everyone.

However, Officer Geo seemed to have one small shortcoming. He was not the best in the world at taking care of his equipment. Our agency always issued us the very best clothing and equipment on the market. Our uniforms; waterproof, insulated boots; waterproof rain suits; goose down vests and coats for those cold nights watching for poachers; and just about every other piece of equipment were top quality. Later, duty belts, portable radios, and even blue lights and sirens for our vehicles became standard issue. When I would go to work with Officer Geo, I would ask, "Where's your ticket book?" or, maybe, "Where's your flashlight?"

"Oh, they're around here somewhere."

"Geo, the tail light is out on your boat trailer."

"Okay, I'll get it fixed." You get the idea. Now, Officer Geo had one of the older boats in the area, but it ran well. It was an old runabout with a windshield only in front of the driver. The outdoor carpet in the bottom of the boat had become so worn and frayed that the passenger (me) was continually blasted in the face with pieces of carpet and glue. At about thirty-five miles per hour, this was a bit uncomfortable. I kept asking Geo to get new carpet put down in the boat and always got the same answer. "Okay, I'll get it done as soon as I can." This went on for several weeks until I had eaten about all the old carpet I wanted. When we had finished our weekend's work one afternoon and had arrived back at Officer Geo's house, I backed my truck up to the boat trailer, hooked it up, and drove back to Greeneville with the boat. The next Monday morning, a trip to town fixed me up with some new outdoor carpet and a can of glue. When I took the boat back home the next weekend, it had a new and much more comfortable floor in it.

Not long before I started working with Officer Geo, the agency decided to join the modern era and issue us better firearms. Most of us were not unhappy to say good-by to the old snub-nosed, aluminum frame .38's. Some of the officers' pistols wouldn't even fire a cartridge. Now we were issued brand new Smith & Wesson, Model 66, .357 Mag. stainless steel revolvers. Boy, what an upgrade!

These pistols were state-of-the-art at the time and began to bring us in line with most other officers in the area of firepower. Of course we had to qualify on the range with the new weapons, but, after a little practice, we managed to get everyone certified with the new pistols. There were no accidents, and soon almost everybody was at least reasonably comfortable with their ability to use these big revolvers.

I guess we had worn the new firearms, complete with their new security holsters, for about a year or so when I went to work Cherokee Lake with Officer Geo one day. I noticed that the safety snap on his holster was broken; it would not keep the pistol from falling out of the holster if the wearer bent over at the waist. "Geo, better get your holster fixed or you're going to have trouble."

"Okay." This routine, again, went on for two or three more weekends without his getting the holster fixed. Then one day we went to the lake as usual. We had been checking boats and fishermen for a couple of hours when we pulled up to a boat with three fishermen in it. There were fishing lines in the water all around their boat so Officer Geo turned off our boat motor to prevent cutting their lines. After we had checked the men's fishing licenses, life jackets, and registration, we pushed off from their boat and snagged one of the lines on the foot of our motor. No big deal. Officer Geo just raised our motor out of the water and leaned over the back of our boat to free the line. The next things I heard were clunk, clunk, splash, uuuuuhhh! That new Smith & Wesson revolver was now on the bottom of Cherokee Lake. We were only about thirty feet off the lake bank, and the water was only about fifteen feet deep at the place where the pistol went down. However, that wasn't much better than being out in the middle of the lake in a hundred feet of water as far as Officer Geo was concerned. In all probability, his firearm was long gone, never to be seen again.

I think Officer Geo had to pay the agency for the pistol before they would issue him another one. Now, some stainless steels are magnetic and can be picked up by a magnet. These pistols were made out of this type of stainless steel, so Officer Geo borrowed a large, very strong magnet from one of the boat docks and made many trips back to the location of the "accident" to drag for the lost firearm. After about six weeks and many, many drags with no luck, a miracle happened right there on Cherokee Lake. When Officer Geo pulled the magnet into his boat one last time, there was his pistol firmly stuck to it. Except for the wooden grips, this firearm seemed to be in pretty good shape. With a thorough cleaning and some new grips, it was almost as good as new. Talk about one happy wildlife officer! Now the Good Lord didn't cause the shootin' iron to swim to the surface like He did the axe head in ancient times, but, I do believe He guided the magnet to it on the bottom of the lake. Miracles still happen!

21

Midnight Kill. Noon Check-in

To everything there is a season,
and a time to every purpose under the heaven.
A time to kill, a time to heal. — Ecclesiastes 3:1, 3a

Sometimes I felt that my agency was slow to come into the world of modern law enforcement, but that may not have been entirely accurate. As I've already told you, our clothing and some equipment were and still are state of the art. However, we were slow in getting things like blue lights and sirens for our vehicles, portable radios, handcuffs, pepper spray, body armor, and a few other things that would make our job a little safer. I think the feeling was that we shouldn't look too much like deputies and policemen. We were supposed to be different. Well, we were different because we were charged mainly with enforcing wildlife and boating laws, but we still dealt with the same law breakers as the other law enforcement departments. Although we didn't go out looking for speeders and such, we did have full arrest powers and could use them to protect the public in case of an emergency. Most violators didn't care whether our uniform was green, blue or purple. They just saw us as a threat to their freedom and sometimes reacted violently to any attempts to take away that freedom. That's why I didn't mind getting chewed out every now and then for wearing body armor or for carrying handcuffs. Better a little chewing than getting hurt by some thug. Now, thankfully, our officers are as well-equipped as those from any other department.

In the fields of forensics and technology, our agency was always willing to adopt the latest methods of crime-solving. I have already talked about the diffusion blood tests that we used to determine the identity of blood samples taken at a crime scene. This test was an immuno-diffusion process whereby the blood samples to be tested were injected into a gel medium and compared to samples of known blood identity. The unknown blood serum would react with a known anti-serum to form a white precipitate if the blood was from the same animal as the anti-serum. This test was one hundred percent accurate and could not be questioned in court. We could also testify with the same accuracy that a blood sample was not from a certain animal. For example, if the defendant said he had been killing hogs that day, we could say for sure that the blood on his boots was not hog blood. We convicted a lot of poachers with this process, but, of course, DNA testing has made most of these type tests obsolete. I also was given the opportunity to study under one of the best law enforcement officers in Tennessee at Walter State Community College. He taught me how to identify different hair samples from animals and people. Hair from each different animal is unique and specific to that particular animal. Thus, one deer hair was all it took to prove that a person was in possession of a deer. The professor also taught me how to identify different firearms, bullet markings, and firing pin markings. My testimony on these subjects was accepted in all the courts in which I was called to testify. Because of my background in chemistry, I could perform almost any laboratory analysis and testify in court about the results. I was even able to assist other departments with some of these tests and analyses.

One of the problems that has plagued most wildlife officers who deal with deer is the poacher who would kill a deer the night before the season opened and attempt to check it out the next morning after the season had opened. In Tennessee, as well as most states, all big game (deer, bear, boar, and turkey) had to be checked in by agency personnel or their representative at a designated checking station. A harvest tag would then be given to the hunter to show that he could now legally possess the deer. Remember, I told you that all wildlife in Tennessee belongs to the citizens of the state. Usually the violator would have a nice buck located on private land and he sure didn't want anyone else to get "his" deer the next day. Therefore, he would spotlight it or moonlight it before legal hunting hours. He would wait until several deer had been checked out the next morning at the designated checking station, and then would bring in his deer to be checked out. Many of these poachers were extremely hard to catch because, if they knew what they were doing, it was almost impossible to determine how long the deer had been dead. As this became more and more of a problem around the country, universities and laboratories began to try to develop a method of determining the time of death for deer. However, we couldn't do anything that would destroy the deer in case it was taken legally. Most hunters frowned upon any agency personnel mangling their trophy deer head just to see when it was killed. For several years, no reliable test was developed. We just couldn't go to court and say with any accuracy how long a deer had been dead. However, with computers becoming smaller, faster, and more reliable, someone got the idea to use several of the time-of-death tests, combine the data, and analyze it on a computer. Three tests were selected as being the most accurate and reliable. One was to insert a thermometer deep into the deer's brain cavity and measure the temperature. The brain temperature drops uniformly for several hours after death. The second test was to measure the diameter of the deer's eye pupil. The eye pupil will dilate at death and gradually close into an oval shape over time after the deer dies. This closure takes about twelve hours to be complete and is pretty accurate when plotted against time. The third test was an electric stimulus test. A pulsating electric current is applied to various points on the deer's skin. The muscles of a recently killed deer will contract quickly and rapidly in response to the electric current, causing the deer's skin to jerk and twitch. The longer the deer has been dead, the less response will be observed when the current is applied to sensitive areas around the eye and mouth. Results from all three tests could be fed into a computer programmed to analyze them, and the computer would then give us a pretty accurate time of death for the deer. We could be sure of the time the deer had been killed within a couple of hours. This was a big help in making cases against night hunters who tried to claim their deer was taken legally during daylight hours.

One opening day, I was at one of our more popular checking stations at about ten o'clock in the morning. A young man came driving up with a really nice eight point buck in the back of his truck. Now, you need to understand that most deer hunters like to show off a nice deer that they have taken. There is certainly nothing wrong with that. If they have done everything legally and in the spirit of fair chase, they can be proud of their trophy. However, most poachers like to show off their ill-gotten deer too. It's just no fun to kill a deer if you can't drive around with it on your vehicle in plain sight and brag about it. That's why this young man brought his deer to the checking station. He wanted folks to see it and to see what a mighty hunter he was. Some of our biologists were also at the checking station that day to collect data from the deer that were brought in. When they put this man's deer on the scales to weigh it, I noticed that it was extremely stiff. Rigor mortis was at its peak, indicating that the deer had been dead at least several hours. A check of the deer's eye pupils told me that I should investigate its time of death a little further. The pupils were almost closed, indicating that the deer had been dead for about twelve hours. I measured the brain temperature and, then, moved the deer over to my truck. There, I connected an electrode to one of the spark plugs on the engine and started the truck. When I touched the electrode to the lips, corners of the eyes, and other sensitive places on the deer's face, there was absolutely no response. Nothing. Not a single twitch or movement. This deer had been dead a long time! I already knew that, but the tests proved it. When all the data was fed into the computer, it gave us a time of death at about eleven or twelve o'clock on the previous night. Remember, we could be off by an hour or so, but there was no doubt that the deer was killed well before opening time that morning. The young man (I won't call him a hunter) vehemently denied that he had shot the deer too early and maintained that it had been dead only a couple of hours. Thanks to these new tests, I had no hesitation in writing him a citation for hunting in closed season or in confiscating the deer.

The judge listened closely to our testimony about the time of death and how we determined it. He agreed with us that the facts presented in this case were indisputable and found the young man guilty on all charges. He paid several hundred dollars in fines and court costs and lost the deer too. The trophy head was mounted and donated to the Greene County Museum where it resides to this day. This young man killed the deer on his family farm and could have taken it home with him that night. Probably, no one would have found out about his late night hunting trip and he would not have been arrested. I guess he just had to show off his "trophy" and his ego got him in trouble.

Word about cases like this spreads rapidly around both legal and illegal hunting circles. It wasn't long before people were commenting on this case and a couple of others we had made. When officers from any department go to court with good, strong cases based on scientifically proven evidence, it goes a long way to helping discourage other would-be violators from committing similar crimes. They realize that, if they're caught, they're as good as convicted. We have to be smarter than the crooks and to stay ahead of them in technology. Thanks research and development guys.

22

Community Crime Watch Spotlighters

Enter not into the path of the wicked,
and go not in the way of evil men. For they sleep not,
except they have done mischief. — Proverbs 4:14, 16a

Wildlife officers' problems with catching night hunters can be caused by many different factors. For one thing, the violators are mobile and extremely hard to catch. There is almost always a vehicle involved, and sometimes the driver is not inclined to stop for blue lights. They have been known to try to run over the officers in order to evade arrest. For another thing, there are six hundred twenty-six square miles in Greene County and only two wildlife officers to patrol such a big area. We were spread pretty thin, to say the least. We might watch a field every night for a week, and the poachers would be spotlighting only a couple of miles away. We had to rely heavily on information given to us by concerned citizens in order to determine the most likely places to watch for violations to occur. Many times folks were reluctant to give us information because the poachers were neighbors or because they were afraid that the bad guys would come back and "burn their barns down." I never even once heard of any barns or other buildings being burned, but I can understand a person wanting to protect his property. Sometimes, sportsmen or land owners would get so fed up with this wildlife thievery that they would give us information that we could really use to nab the poachers. That was when we might ask for assistance from other wildlife officers and set up "details" to concentrate on a certain problem area. We might have officers watching a field or two and have catch-vehicles in place for several nights in a row. As I mentioned earlier, Friday and Saturday nights were usually the best to work because many of the poachers like to make the rounds of the local night-clubs to get their courage up. After a few drinks, they would feel brave enough to go out and "shoot some deers." If everything worked right for us, then we might end up with a situation like the one I described in Chapter 12. However, these successes were few and far between; we would get a call about spotlighting, but, by the time we got to the area, the violators were long gone. Or the information would be so old that it was impossible to use. Still we tried to follow up on every lead because any information that we received had the possibility of leading to the arrest of a poacher.

Early in my career, when most of the deer were concentrated in a small part of Greene County near the wildlife management area, we didn't have nearly as big a territory to watch as later on when the deer population had spread throughout the whole county. We only had a few fields on back roads in the southern part of the county near the mountains to worry about. As the deer population grew, so did our poaching problems. Soon, north, south, east, or west; it didn't matter. The good ol' boys could poach almost anywhere. We began getting calls about night hunters from all over the county, especially the north and west areas. Just like before, we would catch a few now and then but really didn't do much to slow down any illegal hunting. Poaching remained a serious problem.

In the previous chapter, I discussed the use of forensic technology to aid law enforcement. I purposely omitted the use of aircraft because I wanted to save that for this chapter. Since the early 1970's, the agency has had an airplane based in Middle Tennessee. It wasn't used for much except to transport agency personnel or to pick up and deliver supplies quickly. We rarely saw it in East Tennessee; I guess we were just too far from home and the pilot didn't like to fly in the mountains after dark. Then, someone came up with the idea that an airplane could be used to watch for spotlighters at night. An observer in the plane could easily see someone on the ground shining a bright spotlight into a field. In theory, this should work well if the poachers didn't hear the airplane and figure out that it was an "eye in the sky." Because air patrol was new and hadn't been publicized much, it took a while for the spotlighters to figure out what the airplane was doing circling around overhead. Then, too, if they had been at the bars for a while, they were a little slow to think about any wardens in the sky. The air patrols worked pretty well in Middle and West Tennessee. Officers arrested quite a few poachers with the help of the airplane. However, we didn't have nearly as much success in East Tennessee. It was difficult to get the aircraft to fly for us very often, probably because of the danger of night-flying in mountainous terrain. Also, when the airplane did come to East Tennessee it would try to cover a large part of the area in one night. We might sit out in the truck all night and the plane would fly over us only a couple of times. I think we would have had better success by just concentrating on two or three counties instead of trying to cover fifteen or sixteen counties in one night. But I didn't make those decisions. When the airplane did come to fly for us, all officers had to be out working that night. We would usually set up somewhere out of sight and wait and wait and wait. Like I said, maybe once or twice during the night, the plane would actually fly over us.

During one of these air patrols, I made a rather interesting spotlighting case that had nothing, really, to do with the airplane. It was up in the sky somewhere over East Tennessee and all the officers were scattered around in their counties waiting for some action. I was hidden in the back of a church cemetery in the western part of Greene County. I picked this place because we knew that this was a good area for spotlighters. I think the time was well after midnight and the airplane had flown over me once. I was about half asleep when something woke me up. Across the highway from where I was hidden, I saw a small pick-up truck driving very slowly on a side road. All of a sudden, a very bright spotlight came on and lit up the field I was watching. The passenger made several sweeps across this field with the light and then handed it to the driver. He shined the light all over the field on the other side of the road. The truck drove out onto the highway and turned around. On the way back to where I first saw them, they shined both fields again. I radioed for the airplane, but it wasn't anywhere close. Neither were there any other wildlife officers within about twenty miles of me. This stop was going to be up to me alone. After the suspect's truck had topped a small rise in the road and was out of sight, I pulled out of my hiding place and crossed the highway onto the side road behind the spotlighters. I was running blackout with no lights on to keep them from seeing me any sooner than necessary. As I topped the little rise in the road, I saw them shining another field off to my left. They still hadn't seen me and turned onto another side road. I guess they never looked behind them because the truck went on down this road and the occupants shined a few more fields. When the driver started to turn around, I drove onto this second side road and knew I had their truck blocked. They were on a dead end road. There would be no escape! At this point, I radioed the sheriff's department for back up, gave them my location, and told them what was happening. About this time, the truck got pretty close to me but the passenger was still shining the fields around him. Surely they had to see me. There I was, sitting right in front of them in a big green truck. I guess they were doing their own thing in their own world. Suddenly, their world exploded with my blue lights and my spotlights. Making good use of my loudspeaker, I ordered both the driver and passenger out of the vehicle with their hands raised and in plain sight. Now, the night was very cold, but I didn't care. These guys were going to stand in the middle of the road with their hands up until my back up arrived. Then my world lit up with blue lights. Here came two Greene County Sheriff's cruisers and two Tennessee Highway Patrol cars (They had been just over on Interstate 81). Boy were they a welcome sight. The deputies watched my two prisoners for me and the Highway Patrol guys kept a sharp look out for anyone else who might have been in the area. I inventoried the truck and found the spotlight, two loaded rifles, and a couple of six packs of beer. There were also several empty beer cans in the floorboard. The two spotlighters informed me that they were the neighborhood crime watch patrol and were just checking to make sure everybody was safe. Ha! They still got a couple of citations each and had all their equipment confiscated. No more crime watch patrol for them that night.

At the trial, the two men tried to convince the judge that they were just going about their business of keeping the neighborhood safe from criminals in spite of the fact that they had been drinking, were shining open fields, and were in possession of two loaded rifles. It was also just coincidence that the deer season opened the next day. His Honor didn't believe them any more than I did. The verdict was guilty on all charges. They were assessed several hundred dollars in fines and court costs, their hunting privileges suspended for a year, and all their equipment was confiscated. The judge also barred them from participating in the neighborhood crime watch program.

Many thanks to the Greene County Sheriff's Department and to the Tennessee Highway Patrol for their quick assistance. Those blue lights sure looked good when they came up behind me. It helps to have a good relationship with one's fellow officers. You can see why I always tried to assist them if they needed back up.

23

Thunder on the Lake

And Moses stretched forth his rod toward heaven:
and The LORD sent thunder and hail,
and fire ran along the ground. — Exodus 9:23

As you surely know by now, of all the different things we did as wildlife officers, summer lake work was my least favorite. Not only were the days long and hot, but rough water and sometimes bad weather added to the discomfort of the job. The new officers have it much easier than we did. Why, they even have covered boats that provide them with some shade. They get to wear knit shirts and short pants, too. "Modern technology," again. At least, when we were on routine patrol checking life jackets, fishing licenses, and such, we could take a break every now and then. If we were close to a boat dock, we would motor in for a soda or cold iced tea and spend a few minutes in the air conditioned dock house. Then it was back out into the sun until we reached the next boat dock.

One summer, some of the boat dock owners and camp ground owners on the upper part of Cherokee Lake decided that it would be a big attraction to sponsor a drag boat race on the lake. Now, drag boat races are much like drag races on land. The boats blast off from a line when the starting lights turn green and race against the clock for a certain distance. Usually this distance is either an eighth of a mile or a quarter of a mile to the finish line; and, then, the boats need about that much more distance to slow down and stop. The race on Cherokee Lake was set up so that the starting line was at the back of a big cove near Fall Creek. Spectators would have good seats on the lake bank all around the cove to watch the races. The boats could blast off from the starting line, shoot straight up the cove to the finish line near the mouth of the cove, and, then, have the main part of the lake to slow down and stop. There would be no other boats allowed in the cove so that the drag boats could run without fear of hitting someone else. That all sounded safe enough and should have worked well. There was only one small problem. What could be done about the boat traffic out on the main part of the lake? The drag boats easily reached speeds of over two hundred miles per hour and looked more like rockets coming out of the cove than boats. They were about as easy to steer as a .50 cal. machine gun bullet after it has been fired. If anything happened to be in their way before they stopped, there would be a big wreck. The race was being held on a Sunday afternoon and it was not hard to picture all the pleasure boats, jet skis, and fishermen running up and down the lake. Maybe traffic on the main lake wasn't such a small problem after all.

"Oh, well. No big deal. We'll let those officers who regularly patrol the lake handle it. They really don't have much else to do, and, besides it would be good public relations for them."

Problem solved! Guess who was assigned to be the traffic cop for the race. Yep, just me. One race, one officer, one boat, no problem. I suppose it was kind of like the old Texas Ranger tale (one riot, one Ranger). What a way to spend a Sunday afternoon! I was running back and forth from one side of the race track to the other trying to explain to irate boaters why they couldn't go where they wanted to go. You would have thought I had ruined their whole day just because I held them up for a few minutes while a drag boat was running. We did let traffic go through between races. Anyway, the afternoon wore on, the sun was hot, and the waves were rough. I couldn't even take a break and go get a big ol' glass of iced tea.

Then, about four o'clock or so, I noticed a few small clouds building up behind me back toward the west. Still, the boats kept racing. A short time later, the clouds were getting bigger and were turning dark. Still, the boats kept racing. A few more minutes and I began to hear thunder rumbling off in the distance. Still, the boats kept racing. The thunder got a little closer and a few rain drops began to fall. Still, the boats kept racing. All of a sudden, lightning struck the top of a hill up the lake a mile or so and it began to rain harder. Just a typical summer afternoon thunder shower and still, the boats kept racing. By about five o'clock, lightning was dancing all over the hilltops around me and rain was coming down in sheets. Still, the boats kept racing. It was unbelievable that the officials hadn't stopped the races because of all the lightning. I don't think there was anyone left to watch the boats run; they were all safely in their vehicles. About that time, lightning hit directly on the bank right behind my boat. There was smoke, fire, and tree limbs everywhere. I may have been seeing things, but it appeared that even the water was on fire. Still, the boats kept racing.

I immediately promoted myself to agency supervisor and issued a field order (or lake order, in this case) for me to scrub this mission and return to headquarters. I didn't think I would be fired for leaving the races and I sure didn't care if I got chewed out for it. A reprimand was much better than being fried in a boat. A flip of the ignition switch and the big Chevy I/O engine in my boat came to life. I shoved the throttle forward as far as it would go and headed for safer waters. The last I saw of the drag boat races, the boats were still running. I had put the boat in the water at a dock down the lake so I headed in that direction at maximum rpm. Since the storm was coming from the other direction, that got me out in front of the lightning a little bit, but the rain was still pouring down. I switched on the bilge pumps, got down behind the windshield, and ran for cover. A few minutes later, I was tied up safely at the dock and was inside the dock house with that glass of iced tea. Do I believe in guardian angels? You bet I believe in guardian angels. In fact, I think I had several watching over me that day.

At about the same time that I left them, the races were finally suspended due to the storm. I'll never know why it took the race officials so long to call things off. They certainly put many people's lives in danger by waiting so long. While the workers were in the water removing all the electronic gear, lightning struck close enough to them to send several men to the hospital for medical treatment. All the lights and timing equipment were also burned to a crisp. I think the races were rescheduled a month or so later after the company bought all new equipment. No one ever mentioned the fact that I chose not to be struck by lightning that day. I guess my bosses were glad I saved the state equipment and got the boat safely home. My field (lake) promotion didn't last long and I went back to being a regular wildlife officer. That was okay with me, and, even better, that was the one and only drag boat race I was ever assigned to work.

24

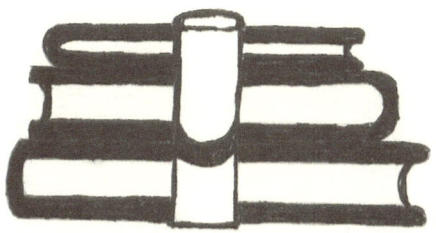

I Guess I Shoulda Stayed in School

If a man have a stubborn and rebellious son,
which will not obey the voice of his father:
Then shall his father lay hold on him and bring him out
unto the elders of his city. — Deuteronomy 21:18-19

This book is dedicated to the memory of U.S. Forest Service Officer Steve Bowman. Steve was assigned as the law enforcement officer for the Nolichucky District of the Cherokee National Forest in and around Greene County. He worked tirelessly with all law enforcement agencies and departments in East Tennessee to fight crime near the national forest. I do not know of a single officer who didn't welcome Steve's help whenever he needed federal assistance. Steve would volunteer for any assignment and was willing to go anywhere in East Tennessee to help with a case. I was privileged to work closely with him in Greene County for several years. He and his wife, Gail, lived in Greene County so I was lucky to have him around much of the time. He helped me with many cases and called me in to work many others that involved state violations. For several years, Steve and I led the whole state of Tennessee in the number of big game cases that we prosecuted. Part of his work as the forest service officer involved the location and destruction of marijuana fields on or near the national forest. He regularly flew with National Guard and Tennessee Highway Patrol pilots to find the fields and then would come back to help cut the marijuana and burn it. It was on one of these flights that Steve's career came to a tragic end. He and a National Guard pilot were flying a "Huey" helicopter in a remote area of Carter County when they were caught in a severe summer thunderstorm. A violent downburst of wind hit the helicopter and blew it into the side of a mountain. The area was so remote that they weren't found for three days. Of course, neither officer survived. They were both killed on impact with the mountain. A distinguished thirteen year law enforcement career was "10-7."

Steve was one of those officers who had the ability to sense when and where a violation might take place. He always seemed to be in the right place at the right time. In this chapter and in Chapter 26, I'll tell you about two such cases that we worked together in Greene County. This first case involved a juvenile deer poacher. One fall night, Steve and I happened to be on patrol in the Houston Valley area of the county. Someone gave Steve information that a deer had been shot from the road and also gave him a description of the pick-up truck involved. Steve radioed me to meet him and advised me of the situation. We got together in his vehicle and began our search for the offending truck. For a while, it seemed that everywhere we went, we just missed it. Folks would tell us that they had seen it, but it had left the area a few minutes before we got there. Up and down the valley we went, for what seemed like half the night. We were always right behind the poacher, but just couldn't catch up to him. Finally, about midnight, we saw the truck parked at a house below a side road. It was barely visible because the road bank dropped off steeply into a little hollow between two hills. There appeared to be someone outside the house at the back of the truck. I guess, this person didn't see us up on the road because Steve was able to make a quick u-turn and get into the driveway before he could escape to the safety of the house. When we began questioning this person, it became evident that he was a juvenile so we had to proceed carefully with our investigation. He admitted that he had been driving the truck that night but denied knowing anything about any deer poaching. However, there was a large amount of what appeared to be deer hair and blood in the back of the truck. I took samples of both for further analyses while Steve gave the young man the required Miranda warning. I also found a rifle behind the seat and seized it for evidence. We had enough probable cause to charge the young man, so he was issued citations for possessing a deer in closed season and for hunting from a public road.

As it turned out, we were just beginning our investigation into this case. Usually, when a juvenile was involved, one of the first things that I did was to talk to the principal of the school he attended. One can get a lot of good background information this way. Most principals and teachers were willing to help us any way they could. This boy's principal was no exception. He told us that the juvenile rarely came to school, was failing every subject he was taking, and usually ended up in in-school-suspension if he bothered to come to class at all. This information would prove to be key to our case in court. I also learned that the young man was sometimes living with an adult woman who was not a family member and had stolen some checks from her. It seems he also bounced a few of them around town a couple of weeks before we became involved with him. My analyses of the hair and blood sample from the truck proved them to be deer hair and deer blood. Also the rifle had been recently fired on the night the alleged poaching occurred. I felt like we had a pretty good case to take to court. The young man didn't have a hunting license and the deer season was closed so there was no way he could legally possess fresh deer or parts of a deer. Remember, hair and blood are considered, by law, to be parts of an animal.

On the morning of the trial, Steve and I were in juvenile court bright and early with our evidence all ready to present to the judge. The defendant and his mother were also there along with the "other woman" with whom the boy was living. We presented our case to the court including the hair and blood samples taken from the truck and the rifle. Then the defense had its turn. The other woman arrogantly testified that this young man was the finest person she had ever known and that he was a model student in school. She said that he made straight A's in his classes and was hardly ever absent. Surely he couldn't be guilty of such a terrible thing as poaching a deer. She conveniently did not mention that the boy had stolen her checks and written a few "hot" ones around town. For rebuttal, I produced the boy's school attendance record, his grade sheet, and his suspension record. I could see that the judge seemed very interested in this part of my testimony. After both the prosecution and the defense had rested, the judge retired to his chambers for a few minutes to consider his decision. We only had a short wait in the courtroom before the judge returned.

The bailiff called out, "All rise for the honorable judge. Thank you. You may be seated." His Honor had the defendant rise and stand before him at the bar. The boy's attitude had been rather arrogant throughout the trial and now he faced the judge with somewhat of a smirk on his face. "Young man, you were in my court two weeks ago on these bad check charges that the officers mentioned. I was not impressed with your behavior then and I'm certainly not impressed now. I ordered you to attend school regularly and to bring your grades up to passing ones. You have done neither. You were also supposed to live at home and to observe the curfew I set for you. Again, you haven't done that. These officers have proven to me that you were out shooting deer when you should have been home studying. Therefore, I find you guilty of all charges and hereby declare you to be delinquent before this court. Deputy, put him in a cruiser right now and don't stop until you are behind the gates of the juvenile correction facility. Young man, you are not to even go home for a toothbrush or a change of clothes. Go with this deputy immediately and may God have mercy on you."

The smirk on the defendant's face suddenly disappeared, and the young man literally fell to the floor, shaking and sobbing. He had to be helped up and carried out of the courtroom and placed into the cruiser to begin his journey toward rehabilitation. This is a sad case because it involves a young life that was headed in the wrong direction. This person spent several years in custody before being released back into society. I don't know what ever happened to him, and we can only pray that his time in the detention center helped him to become a decent citizen of Greene County. Steve and I did what we thought was best for this boy in order to get him the help he needed to turn his life around. I hope we succeeded.

25

Bucky Joins the Marines

So I prophesied as He commanded me,
and the breath came into them, and they lived,
and stood upon their feet, an exceeding great army.
— Ezekiel 37:10

All of the agencies and departments that I worked with had a good working relationship with the military personnel in our area. For Greene County, that meant the Army Reserve's 844 Engineer Battalion and the Army National Guard's 278 Armored Cavalry Regiment, but we also worked closely with other military units. I have already told about the 101st Airborne EOD guys coming to our rescue and helping to dispose of some dangerous explosives. My agency also worked with the Coast Guard and its auxiliary on boating safety programs, boat inspections, and other water-related activities. However, I guess we were most often doing something with the National Guard and the Reserve units. Both helped to construct the Greeneville-Greene County firing range, and we all used it for firearms training. Both groups were also very willing to let us "borrow" surplus or unused equipment if we needed something they had. For a long time, I had a camouflage M-1 Abrams Tank cover that we used to hide our trucks when watching for poachers, and I could always round up a few MRE's (Meal, Ready-to-Eat) if we were going to be on a long detail with no burger joints handy. Most officers had at least one pair of Army BDU's (again, Battle Dress Uniform) for use when we didn't want to be seen. Some departments issued them and some didn't, but we could usually get a replacement cap or belt from the Army if they had some extra ones. If I had an unusually large hunter education class, I could use the big tank bay at the National Guard building for a meeting place. So you see, the military and law enforcement have a lot in common and it was only natural that we work together whenever we could. Many departments even used the same military ranking system for their officers. Sergeant, Lieutenant, or Captain was a pretty common way to address a military man or a law enforcement officer. As I explained in Chapter 8, most of the time, we were just one big happy family.

I never had the opportunity to work with the Marines because there just weren't any assigned to this area. But then one day, in the mid 1990's, I met one of the best known Marines of that era. Lieutenant Colonel Oliver North had just retired from the Marine Corps and was working as a public relations representative and field man for a company that sold body armor to military and law enforcement departments. You may recall that Oliver North served as a platoon commander in Vietnam where he received the silver star, bronze star, and two purple hearts. He then became an instructor at Quantico, and later returned to Vietnam where he was promoted to Captain. Colonel North returned to the United States, was promoted to Major, and was assigned to the National Security Council in 1981. He received his final promotion to Lieutenant Colonel in 1983 and remained in the Washington, D.C. area until he retired from the Marine Corps in 1988.

The Greene County Sheriff's Department made arrangements for Colonel North to come to Greeneville to demonstrate the body armor sold by his company. The demonstration was set up at our firing range and all neighboring departments were invited. I took a day's vacation in order to attend. We did not have body armor at that time, but I was interested in buying some for my own use. I think we all met at about 10 A.M. and had lots of fun shooting the vests and watching other demonstrations done by Colonel North. For lunch, he had barbecue catered to the range and invited us all to join him for barbecue sandwiches and all the trimmings. A second invitation was not necessary to get all the officers present to enjoy a good meal. After lunch, there were a few more demonstrations, and then Colonel North was kind enough to shake hands with everyone and to pose for a picture with any officer who wanted one. For some reason, Bucky, our mounted deer (see Chapter 6) was mentioned and the Colonel said that he had heard about using them to catch poachers. He also expressed a wish to see one in action. Well, that was no problem. Officer Steve Bowman lived close by so he just jumped into his truck and ran home to get Bucky. A few minutes later, Bucky was doing his tail wagging and head turning tricks for Colonel North. I think the Colonel was quite as impressed with our demonstration as we were with his, and he spent an hour or so talking about how to trick the bad guys and then catch them. He even conferred a field commission of Lieutenant Colonel on Bucky. Then it was our turn to take Colonel North's picture with the deer. Even though Bucky's Marine Corps career was very short, he showed his versatility by being a good colonel, and a good entertainer as well as a good catcher of poachers.

I don't know if anyone bought any body armor from the Colonel or not, but we sure did have a lot of fun that day. Not only did we meet a well-known Marine Corps officer and get to play with some high tech police apparel, but we had a good time visiting with the other officers in a non-stressful situation. I realize that Colonel North was a little controversial for some folks, but, that day, he was truly an officer and a gentleman with us. I still have my picture taken with him. Bucky still has his, too, I'm told.

Law enforcement is such a stressful occupation that, I think, any time we get together, put our differences aside, and just have a good time, we can relieve some of that stress. That helps us all to do our jobs more efficiently and to be better officers. We all know that better officers make for a better and safer community.

26

Hilltop Deer and Turkeys

Seest thou a man that is hasty in his words?
There is more hope of a fool than of him. — Proverbs 29:20

This will be my last poaching tale. I promise. Poaching doesn't happen only at night as you might remember from Chapter 18. In the case that I'll tell you about here, it occurred on the day before deer season opened in November. A man from another state and his adult son bought a house and some property near the Cherokee National Forest in the Houston Valley area of Greene County. The house was located about a fourth of a mile or so off the main road. It was over one hill and on top of another hill that couldn't be seen from vehicles traveling up and down the road. With national forest all around, it was a dandy location for a poacher. One could just step out the door and shoot whatever came through the back yard. The gun shot would be hard to hear and the game could be quickly hidden or dressed and put in the freezer in a matter of a few minutes. There were plenty of deer and turkey in the area and it wasn't unusual for a bear to drop in now and then. If a person liked wild game, he could eat well pretty much the year around.

Early that fall, we began to get some second hand information that something "funny" was going on at this house. Because the house was out of sight and because the only access to it was by the narrow driveway, it was difficult to follow up on anything we were told without walking to a hillside in the national forest and then "camping out" to watch the property. We actually did this a couple of times without any success. Officer Steve Bowman did the hiking and camping, but he never saw anything suspicious. We tried to keep our eyes and ears open as best we could because, as deer season approached, we were getting enough information to be pretty sure that the adult son was doing quite a bit of poaching. It seems he was very fond of venison. Then, on the opening day of deer season, I was given some reliable information that, on the previous day, the son had killed a big buck and had hidden it at the house. Still, all I had was hearsay evidence, but I considered it to be worth checking out. I radioed Officer Steve who was in the area and asked him to meet me at an old store building near the Houston Valley Road. I filled him in on what I had been told and we tried to come up with a plan of action that might work.

We finally put together a very complicated plan that would involve some very sophisticated police work. We would just go talk to the son and see what he had to say! Maybe he would slip up and tell us something we could use or maybe there would be some evidence in plain sight. If we had probable cause to be where we were and saw something illegal out in the open, we could use it. I think we used Steve's vehicle and proceeded to the driveway leading from Houston Valley Road to the house. As we approached the driveway, we saw the father at his mailbox down at the road. So much for a surprise arrival. The only thing left to do was to talk to the father. I introduced Steve as the Chief Investigator for the U.S. Forest Service, Nolichucky District (I didn't lie. He was the only one). I introduced myself as the agency's Chief Detective for Greene County (Again, no lie.). We just plainly told him we had information that his son had killed a deer illegally on the previous day and we wanted to talk to him about it.

The father said, "I guess you know all about it so I just as well tell the truth." He told us that, yes, the son had killed the deer and it was at the house. Okay! So far, so good. He said that his son was hunting that morning but should be home before long. He even suggested that we come to the house to wait for him. Things were getting even better. Steve and I followed the man over the hill and up to his house. We parked the vehicle in the yard and started walking toward the door. I looked down and saw some wild turkey feathers scattered around the yard. The more I looked, the more feathers I saw. I picked up some and held them up for Steve to see. He looked back with a big grin that told me he had seen them too. I put a few of the feathers in my pocket and, when we got inside the house, the father said, "I guess you want to know about the turkeys, too."

"Yes, Sir. We were just fixing to ask you about them." The man replied that son had killed three turkeys a week or so earlier and they were in the house too. One was in the refrigerator and two were in the freezer along with the deer meat. Things were still getting better.

We didn't have to wait too long for the son to return from his morning hunt. He wasn't very happy to see us and probably suspected something bad was about to happen. He told us that he hadn't had any luck hunting that morning and then asked what we were doing there. At this point, we advised him of his rights and informed him that his father had told us all about his activities during the past week. Talk about one angry son! He was not happy with Pop at all. He became very uncooperative and even suggested that we had no right to be on their property. "We had probable cause to believe that a crime had been committed here, your dad owns the property and invited us here, we saw evidence in plain sight, and you're out of luck." was our reply. Of course, the son could not produce a hunting license or a harvest tag for the deer and, because turkey season had been closed for about seven months, he couldn't have taken them legally either. Since the father owned the house where the illegal game was located, he became an accessory to the crimes committed by his son. We then advised the father of his rights and began to write the appropriate citations to both men. The son began to get pretty agitated so Steve kept a close eye on him while I did the writing and collected all the evidence. We did this as quickly as possible and hastily retreated to the main road in case the son had another deer rifle handy. We can only guess what the conversation was like between father and son after we left. I heard later that it wasn't too friendly. The deer head with a really big rack was supposed to be at a somewhat shady taxidermist's shop just down the road in the next county. We retrieved it and took all the meat to a freezer where we could store it for evidence. The taxidermist was charged with possessing deer parts without a valid harvest tag. He tried to get a little feisty until we advised him we would be back to inventory the rest of his animals to make sure they were all legal.

I ran the necessary lab tests on the meats to prove that they were deer and turkey. Of course, that's what they were, so along with the turkey feathers I had collected and our harvest tag records, we had a pretty strong court case. The father and the taxidermist forfeited cash bonds and did not contest their charges in court. The son, who was still a little defiant, thought he would take his chances before the judge. Bad decision. He ended up paying heavier fines than the others, but even that didn't change his attitude much. He left the courtroom muttering a few veiled threats about wildlife officers and Greene County courts.

I think this dysfunctional family of father and son left Greene County not long after this incident took place. I don't know where they went, but I can sympathize with their new neighbors. As usual, the meat was given to the Greene County jail. The head with its huge rack of antlers was taken to a taxidermist in Greene County and he also donated the mount to the Greene County Museum. As far as I know, it, too, is still part of their collection. We never did figure out why the father so willingly told us all about his son's illegal activities. I guess the moral of this tale is, if you are going to poach in your own back yard, be sure you can trust your father to keep his mouth shut.

27

Rattler in the Window

At last, it biteth like a serpent and stingeth like an adder.
— Proverbs 23:32

In Tennessee, as well as in many other states, it is illegal to keep a poisonous reptile as a pet. Only licensed zoos, research institutions, and rehabilitation centers can possess these animals and they must have a permit from the state and must provide safe, secure facilities for them. I think the reason for this law is pretty obvious. Some poisonous reptiles can be dangerous to people and can inflict serious injury or death to human beings and other animals. Also, rattlesnakes are sometimes killed for their skins and rattles. These are sold to make clothing accessories and jewelry. Excluding the poisonous varieties, most reptiles and, especially snakes, are quite beneficial to all of us. Even the poisonous ones eat a lot of rats, mice, and insects. There are no better mousers than snakes. That's one reason that it's also illegal to kill a snake in Tennessee. Now before you think that I'm too crazy, let me explain. We fully understand that a person has every right to protect himself and his family from harmful animals. I'm referring to the unnecessary killing of snakes just because they are snakes or for their skins. In East Tennessee, there are only two species of poisonous snakes; the copperhead and the eastern timber rattlesnake. There are no cottonmouth moccasins or other poisonous snakes in the wild around here. Both of these poisonous snakes are rarely seen and really pose no threat to people as long as we take a few precautions when we are out in the open. Make a little noise, watch where you put your hands and feet, and you shouldn't have many problems with snakes. If they know that you're around, you'll never see them because they will quickly leave the area. If you leave them alone, they will leave you alone.

Most people I know really do not like snakes very much and I guess that is Biblical. However, there are a few misguided souls that have a fascination with them or think that having a snake will make him more "macho" than the next guy. This may have been the reason for an incident that occurred in downtown Greeneville. I think that it was one of the Greeneville police officers that asked me one day, "Have you seen that big snake that Mr. D has in his pool hall down on Depot Street?" No, I hadn't seen it but that was my cue to go look for it. I parked my truck on Depot Street and walked the half a block or so to the business establishment for which I was looking. Sure enough, there in the front window, right under the big letters that said "POOL HALL" was a glass cage. In the cage was the biggest eastern diamondback rattlesnake that I had ever seen. It turned out to be well over six feet long and was about as big around as a professional wrestler's arm. Its head was about the size of a blacksmith's fist. Since it was a diamondback rattler, I knew that it was not a local reptile; it had to have come from further south. The cage didn't look very secure to me so I thought backup was in order to make sure we could keep the situation safe. Officer George soon joined me and we went inside to talk to Mr. D, the owner. He said that he had gotten the snake in Alabama and didn't know that it was illegal to have it. We assured him that keeping a poisonous reptile is illegal in Tennessee and that we would have to confiscate it. Another unhappy customer. Mr. D didn't appreciate getting a citation for possessing a poisonous reptile, but he was more than a little upset about losing "his" snake. We took it anyway. The top of the cage was loose and the snake could have escaped any time it wanted. See what I mean about these animals being dangerous to people. We secured the cage and took the snake to a safe facility to hold it until the trial date.

On the day of the trial, Officer George and I arrived at the courthouse bright and early. We carried our evidence into the courtroom and placed it on the judge's bench. For some reason, the courtroom didn't seem to fill up with people like it usually did. When the judge came in, he quickly opened court for business and then said, "GET THIS EVIDENCE OUT OF MY COURTROOM. I'VE SEEN ALL OF IT I NEED TO SEE." The people near the bench quickly cleared the way for us to take the snake out into the hall. Mr. D pled "not guilty" but didn't really have any defense to present. The judge knew the law. We didn't have to offer much testimony except that we found the snake inside the pool hall owned by Mr. D. That put it in his possession. His Honor found the defendant guilty of illegal possession of a poisonous reptile and fined him the minimum fine plus court cost. Mr. D wasn't too happy with the verdict, but he seemed to accept it until he asked judge, "Can I have my snake back now?"

The judge looked at him over his desk and replied, "No, sir, Mr. D. You may not have your snake back. It is hereby placed into the custody of these officers for safe-keeping until it can be turned over to an approved facility."

Mr. D looked at Officer George and me and said, "Well, just keep the old snake, then. It suits your personality, anyway."

The judge added, "That will be an extra ten dollars in fines plus the court cost and you will serve three days in the county jail for contempt of court." See, I told you it's best to leave poisonous snakes alone. They can be dangerous.

The Knoxville Zoo was overjoyed at our contribution to their serpentarium. It turned out that it was a female snake and they needed a girlfriend for a male snake that was already there. Wildlife officers at your service. Always happy to oblige.

28

Bear !

David said, moreover, The Lord ... delivered me out of the paw of the lion, and out of the paw of the bear. — 1 Samuel 17:37

No book written by an East Tennessee game warden would be complete without at least one bear tale.

Author's note: When I use the word "bear" in this chapter, I am referring to the American Black Bear. It is the only species of bear native to Tennessee.

Ever since Daniel Boone carved his famous inscription, "D BOONE CILLED A BAR" on a beech tree near Jonesborough, bear hunting has been a tradition in the Southern Appalachian Mountains. If you think coon hunters and deer hunters are passionate about their sport, try hanging out with a bunch of bear hunters for a while. It will give you a whole new perspective on the meaning of the word "dedicated." Although there have been bear hunters in East Tennessee ever since the settlers first crossed the mountains and found enough flat land on which to build a house, the hunters have not always ended up with a new bear rug and a roast for Sunday dinner. As more and more people moved into the Appalachians, bear habitat began to shrink and bears moved farther and farther back into the rough country. Bears require a lot of territory in which to live and search for food. It is not unusual for a male bear to roam twenty or thirty miles in a day looking for a meal. With the decline in habitat came a decline in bear populations throughout Appalachia. When I went to work in Greene County in the early 1970's, bears were confined to the Smokey Mountain National Park and to the Cherokee National Forest. The chances of anyone seeing a wild bear, much less hunting one, were pretty slim. Although a few early settlers sometimes may have hunted bear for meat (It is quite good when it is cooked right), most hunting is done for sport and usually requires the use of dogs. When a bear track or other sign is found, dogs are turned loose to chase the bear until it is bayed or treed. This type of bear hunting is very similar to coon hunting except that the bear is much bigger, stronger, and faster than a coon. Once the bear has been bayed or treed, the hunters hope to get to it before it can injure or kill the dogs. This is no easy task, since most hunts take place in rugged, mountainous territory. The hunters have to be in good physical condition to follow the dogs. However, the invention of tracking collars for the dogs and CB radios for the hunters made keeping up with the bear somewhat easier. Still, only a few hunters actually follow the dogs through the woods. Most try to get as close as possible to the chase by using the roads and trails that are available in the area and, then, joining the party when the bear is treed.

Now, you folks need to understand that bear hunting in this area is as much a social event as it is a hunting event. Many people, who do not have dogs, like to drive to the hunting areas in order to hear a good chase and to be there when the bear is brought out of the woods. Everyone joins in the fun and in the celebration of a successful hunt. Many a hunting story is swapped while waiting for the dogs to strike a scent and many a can of sausage is shared with fellow hunters or anyone else who may be around at lunch time. These tasty morsels, along with crackers and cheese, make up many a bear hunter's meal while they are in the woods. One day while on patrol during the bear hunt, I drove up to Horsehitch Gap on the Greene Mountain Road.

There were several hunters stopped there listening for dogs on a chase, so I sat in my truck and listened for a while, too. It was about noon and some of the hunters started to open cans of sausage and packages of crackers. There were a few sodas brought out and lunch began. I said to some of the folks standing next to my truck, "If you don't mind, I think I'll just join you. I'm getting kinda hungry, too." I opened a package of crackers, put them on the dashboard of the truck, and then reached into a sack on the seat for a big jar of pickled pig's feet. I forked a nice foot out of the jar, put it on a paper towel, and began to enjoy my lunch. When I looked up, there was nobody standing around my truck any longer and some of the other hunters had driven off "to look for a better listening place." I thought bear hunters were supposed to be tough.

Since most bear hunting is done by chasing the bear with dogs, I guess the dogs should get some recognition, too. There are many different breeds of bear dogs. Some of the most popular are Plotts, Walkers, and Black and Tans, but you might see most any of the large hound breeds in the woods. Occasionally, you might even see an Airedale, bulldog, or Catahoula. If they will tree a bear and fight it, somebody will have one. As with coon dogs, bear dogs are a source of pride for their owners. Each hunter knows his dogs and can identify them by their bark. Some are better at tracking the bear; some are better at running the bear; and some are better at treeing the bear. An owner can, and usually will, brag about his dog doing something better than the others. Good bear dogs, like good trucks, are not cheap. A hunter might pay thousands of dollars for a dog that has the potential to be better than the ones he has. Because these animals are quite valuable, they are not mistreated in any way. They get the best veterinary care and the best food available. A hunter might miss a meal, but his dogs won't. Occasionally a dog may be injured by a bear. Bears are not clumsy. They are unbelievably quick and strong. When they feel threatened, they will protect themselves and this sometimes means that the dogs get the worst end of the chase. I've known hunters to make more than one emergency run to a local veterinarian with a badly mauled dog or two. There is some still-hunting for bear in Tennessee, but it is usually done in conjunction with other hunts that are going on at the same time. If you don't have dogs or hunt with someone who does have dogs, you probably won't be too successful in bagging a bear. In recognition of the importance of dogs in bear hunting, the state of Tennessee exempts them from needing a hunting license or big game license.

As I mentioned at the beginning of this chapter, early in my career, bear hunters were not very successful in Greene County or in many of the other nearby counties. Open seasons were short and took place during the fall when the weather was sometimes very warm. This was a time when the bears were foraging heavily in preparation for their long winter nap and were particularly vulnerable to hunting. Many sow bears were taken on these early hunts and this, of course, contributed to the decline in the number of bears. I think that it was in the early 1980's that biologists came up with a plan to better protect the bear population and to still provide hunting opportunities for those who enjoy this sport. Bear hunting is not allowed in the Smokey Mountain National Park so the bears had a refuge there. Other bear refuges were set up in the Cherokee National Forest to provide safe areas where no hunting is allowed. These refuges alternated with areas open for hunting so that bears could "escape" to a safe haven every now and then. They also provided good den sites and forage areas year around. The hunting season was moved to early December when most of the sow bears were in their dens for the winter. Now, far more male bears would be taken during the hunts than sow bears. This protected the young cubs and the female bears who would be having cubs while in the den. After a few years, we began to notice an increase in the legal bear harvest. The harvest numbers continued to rise slowly for several years indicating that the combination of refuges and later seasons was working. The harvest totals plus data from population surveys soon suggested to the biologists that bear numbers would support a training season that allowed the hunters to run their dogs and chase bear at certain times as long as no bears were harmed. Then after a few more years, we were able to lengthen the taking season by three or four days. Populations have continued to increase to the point where we now have a fairly liberal bear season with most East Tennessee counties open. It is not unusual to see bears in populated areas and even in towns close to the mountains. Some folks even complain about the bears eating their apples and scaring their house pets. That's quite a change from the twenty-nine bears taken statewide in 1951. The record harvest for the entire state of Tennessee was five hundred eighty-one bears taken in 2011. Every year since 2004 the statewide harvest has exceeded three hundred bears. I guess the biologists know what they are doing at least some of the time. Of course, it takes good law enforcement too.

With the longer bear seasons, bear patrols became a little more hassle-free than they used to be. The action was far from non-stop for much of the time. If no fresh tracks were found or if no bears were located, we would just sit around and wait for the next chase. That was a good time to stop at a country store for a soda, a pack of crackers, and a visit with the local folks. Sometimes you can learn a lot about what is going on around the area just by listening to store gossip. Every now and then idle game wardens will think of ways to stir up some action if things are really slow. Some of these bear dogs have good enough noses to smell a bear while riding on the hood or on top of a truck as the hunter drives slowly along a back road or trail in a hunting area. The dog can actually pick up the scent of a bear if it has recently crossed the road or been close to the road. These strike dogs will sound off if they smell a fresh track, and other hunters can then bring more dogs to turn loose for the chase. I've known of some of those idle officers who would use a garden trowel to make scratch-marks on a big tree next to a road. The scratches would look as if a bear had climbed the tree or had clawed the tree as a boundary marker for his territory. "These officers" would pour a liberal amount of bear scent down the side of the tree trunk and onto the ground around the tree. "They" would then hide and listen for some action on the CB radio (We had them, too).

"Hush, boys. Ol' Jake's just found sumpthin' fresh. Yeah, he's really soundin' off. Better get some more dogs up here and check this out. I believe it's really a hot track. Hurry!"

Chuckle. Chuckle.

"Aw, shucks, boys. Don't believe this un'll go after all. Just stay where you are, I guess."

More chuckling. Those idle game wardens would need to make sure their green trucks weren't seen anywhere near the "scent tree" or some bear hunters would get mighty suspicious all of a sudden.

I've talked about deer poaching in several chapters, so maybe I should say something about bear poaching here. As long as there have been bear hunters, there has been bear poaching. Before states passed game laws, it probably wasn't illegal to go out and kill a bear. It might make other hunters or your neighbors angry, but you wouldn't be arrested for poaching. Then, after states began to set open seasons, some folks just couldn't stand to be told that they weren't allowed to hunt at certain times. You know, the personal freedom thing. For my entire career, I had to deal with bear poaching from time to time. Before training seasons, some folks just wanted to run their dogs. Others were bent on killing the bear so they could brag to their friends. Then money came into the picture. The Far East began paying a high price for dried bear gall bladders (They sell for as much as $600 apiece.) for use in some of their potions to make one feel and act younger. Claws, teeth, and hides also bring a good price when sold on the black market. It became profitable to have a bear or its parts in one's possession. Poachers would try to kill a bear late at night or early in the morning when they were least likely to be discovered or reported to the game wardens. We would hear about these incidents, but it was usually too late to make a case good enough to stand up in court. Some folks would also set traps waaay up in the mountains where they were unlikely to be found. These traps were made from fifty-five gallon steel drums and fitted with a sliding trap door. They were baited with honey buns, bacon, chocolate, sardines, or just about anything that a bear could smell. When we located these traps, a little det chord, some C-4 and a couple of blasting caps would render them unusable for much of anything except scrap metal.

The poaching got so bad that an undercover operation conducted by several state and federal agencies was begun in order to address the problem. Both state and federal officers worked undercover for two years to collect evidence on the illegal possession and sale of bear parts. "Operation Smokey" covered several states and the Smokey Mountain National Park. One day I received a message from headquarters to meet the chief of law enforcement at the Crossville airport at noon on the next day. All morning, as I drove to Crossville, I tried to figure out what I had done wrong that might get me a reprimand or get me fired. However, when the meeting with the chief took place, I was given a briefing on "Operation Smokey" and was informed that a "roundup" of all the individuals who had been indicted on federal and state charges would take place on a certain date. The chief advised me in no uncertain terms that, if I leaked any information about the operation to anyone, he would personally see to it that I would not work another day as a Tennessee wildlife officer. On the afternoon before the roundup was to take place, all the enforcement officers from the areas involved were quickly taken to a motel in Knoxville and sequestered for the night. At four o'clock the next morning, we began a sweep to arrest a number of individuals in Tennessee and several other states. They all had been indicted on federal or state charges involving the illegal sale and possession of bear parts. Most were convicted in federal court and paid heavy fines. Some had their hunting privileges suspended on federal land, and, I think, a few may have served some jail time. The result of "Operation Smokey" was that most bear poaching came to a screeching halt for a while.

Poaching will never be completely eliminated as long as there are animals to poach, but some of the bear hunters actually began to buy into the agency's conservation programs. They saw that, if they wanted to keep on hunting, they must conserve the resource (the bears). Bears are now being reintroduced into Big South Fork and other areas of the state where they once thrived. Let's hope that there will be room in this state for both man and wildlife for many years to come.

29

The Mountain Haint That Ain't

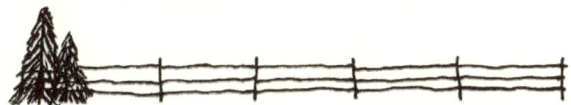

But they were terrified and affrighted,
and supposed that they had seen a spirit. — Luke 24:37

Most folks rarely see their local wildlife officer, much less get a chance to talk to him or ask him a question. Unless you are a sportsman who hunts and fishes a lot, or unless you attend a hunter education class or a program given by an officer, you probably only pass a green truck on the highway every once in a while. There are usually two officers assigned to each county so, with counties as large as Greene, they are not able to spend much time in any one area. If there aren't many violations occurring in some parts of a county, the officer will probably concentrate on areas with the higher incidents of crime. This means that, unless you are breaking the law or unless you contact the officer directly, you may not have many opportunities to meet him. Certainly, more officer contact with the public would be better for everyone, but with so few wildlife officers, this situation is not likely to change.

However, for many years, the agency has done one thing more than any other in East Tennessee to put wildlife officers in touch with the public. That single event is the wildlife exhibit at the Appalachian Regional Fair in Gray, Tennessee. For as long as I can remember this exhibit has been one of the most popular attractions at the fair. The Appalachian Fair folks have always bent over backwards to accommodate us and to ensure that we can have a first rate exhibit. We have our own building that is constructed to provide comfort and safety for the animals on display and to provide easy access to the exhibit for the fair visitors. Most people are not too happy about receiving a citation or being told they can't do something, but we very rarely had any negative comments about the fair exhibit. During the time that I was working, about seven or eight thousand people visited the fair each night. Most of them came through the wildlife exhibit; some of them more than once. That meant forty-five to fifty thousand people saw our exhibit in the week that the fair was open. Ninety-nine plus percent of them left the building after enjoying a positive visit with the agency. That's what good public relations is all about.

Wildlife officers spend many hours each year readying the exhibit for opening day. Repairs to the building and cages have to be made. Sometimes new exhibits are put up. Hand-out material has to be picked up and taken to the fairgrounds. All of these things take up a lot of the officers' time, but, probably, getting all the wildlife rounded up and getting them settled into their new homes for a week takes more time than anything else. We always tried to have examples of most of the small game animals and aquatic life that folks might see in East Tennessee. Due to space limitations and for safety reasons, we did not display any big game animals. No deer, bear, boar, turkey, bobcats, or black panthers. They are difficult to obtain and can't be confined in small cages like we have in the wildlife building. Any wild animal can hurt you, but the bigger they are, the more dangerous they can be. For these reasons we confined our displays to squirrels, rabbits, quail, foxes, 'possums, raccoons, doves, ducks, geese, and the like. We also had a wide variety of aquatic life such as turtles, frogs, salamanders, and most species of fish found in East Tennessee waters. I guess the most popular exhibit was the snake cage (actually, it was a secure glass box). As you might have gathered from the last chapter, some folks have an attraction to snakes, from a safe distance. There were always rattlesnakes, copperheads, blacksnakes, and several other varieties on display. To accommodate all these wild animals, we had to make sure that the tanks and cages were constructed and placed properly so that the animals would be safe and comfortable. The already unhappy little creatures needed to be away from human contact as much as possible to minimize the stress on them, but they still needed to be visible to the fair visitors. We also had to protect these visitors from the animals. You would think folks would know better than to stick their fingers into a raccoon or fox cage, but this was not always the case. People do strange things, sometimes.

Most folks found the wildlife exhibit to be a pleasant experience. They could pick up the new hunting or fishing guide or other material of interest to them. They could ask the officers questions about rules and regulations or about things they just wanted to know pertaining our great outdoors. City kids and adults could actually see live animals and learn about their habitat. The fair exhibit requires a lot of work and many hours are spent getting the exhibit ready and, then, manning it while the fair is open. We all enjoy the work, though, and are happy to do something so positive toward the public.

Manning the exhibit for the week that the fair was open usually required two or three officers each night. We took turns and worked only one or two nights during the week. We would come in early, before the fair opened, to feed and water the animals and to spruce up the exhibit for the coming flood of visitors. One year, on the day I was assigned to work the exhibit, we got everybody fed and all the other chores done a little early. With nothing really to do until opening time, we were just walking around the building, making sure everything was in order when we noticed an empty cage over in one corner. For some reason, we were not able to find the animal that should have been in that cage. Well, you know what they say about an idle mind. I just couldn't let that cage sit there without putting it to good use. Now, each cage is labeled with a sign showing the type of animal that is in it, but the empty one didn't have a label of any kind on it. I checked our supplies and quickly found the blank sign that I wanted. With a few strokes of a "Sharpie" pen, we now had an "East Tennessee Mountain Haint" in the empty cage. For you flatlanders, a haint is a ghost. To make things a little more realistic, I buried a gallon plastic jug in the wood shavings in the cage so that only the mouth of the jar showed. It looked sort of like a den or nest in the shavings. We also rigged up a stick under the shavings near the jug and tied a string to it. We ran the string out of sight to a place where we could pull it and make the shavings move like something alive was actually there. Idle minds at work. As it turned out, the "haint" cage was even more popular than the snake cage that year. There would be fifty or sixty people gathered around it at any given time trying to see a mountain haint.

A little pull on the string and we would hear, "Oh, it's in there. I see something moving."

We were asked many questions like, "Where did you get him?"

"We caught him (or is it a "her") about midnight one night in a cemetery up in Carter County."

"Well, what does he eat?"

"We're not sure. We haven't had to feed him yet." Some folks would want to know if he was really in there. "We think he is. He mostly sleeps in the daytime and then comes out more at night." On and on, the questions came. All night long. By the time the fair closed for the night, we were worn out, but I think the East Tennessee mountain haint far surpassed the record for the most visitors at any one exhibit. Unfortunately, we were never able to capture one again. We had to make do without a haint the next year, but a lot of folks asked about him. We assured them that he was "alive" and doing well wherever he was.

After the fair is over, we return all the animals to wherever we got them. At first, a lot of the animals were trapped from the wild so they were returned to the wild. Then we began to make use of zoos, rehabilitation centers, universities and the like as a source for the animals. These were returned to the people from whom we borrowed them. Animals that were used to being around people did much better when the building filled up with folks wanting to get a look at them. They were much easier and safer to transport both to and from the fair. This made shutting down the exhibit a lot quicker too. Until we went to get the mountain haint out of his cage, that is. We couldn't find him. We looked in all the cages, in every part of the building, and even searched the fairgrounds for him. He was nowhere to be found. This was quite disturbing to us because we were always so careful to take good care of the animals in order to keep them safe until they were released or returned home. Another search of the entire fairgrounds turned up nothing. That haint just could not be found anywhere. After many hours of looking for him, we just had to accept the fact that our most popular fair exhibit was not going to be located. We could come to only one conclusion. The East Tennessee mountain haint....ain't!

Epilogue

The grace of our LORD Jesus Christ be with you all. Amen. —
Revelation 22:21

Most of the tales in this book are, at least, a little bit humorous. I meant for them to be that way. The Bible says that laughter is good for the soul. Some of the tales are serious and a couple of them could have been dead serious. Let us not forget that law enforcement is a dangerous profession. In 2013, sixty-seven officers in the United States lost their lives while trying to "protect and serve." That's sixty-seven too many. There is even some risk involved in almost everything we do, but you must remember that officers are armed and have the authorization to use deadly force in some situations. We are also dealing with people who have no respect for the law or for the rights of others. Some even want to die and want the police to take their lives for them. I don't know how much my wife and kids thought about the fact that, when I went to work, I might not come home again. I really didn't want to know. I didn't dwell on that possibility each time I got into the green truck either, but it's always in the back of every officer's mind. It helps to keep you alert.

We receive the best training possible to keep us and the public as safe as possible. This training becomes second nature and helps an officer to react properly in a dangerous situation. In my thirty years as a wildlife officer, there were only about three times that I drew my weapon with the thought that I might have to fire it. Thank God, I never had to pull the trigger. Unfortunately, there are a few officers who can't say that. We may have only a half a second to decide what to do in a confrontation, but the courts have years to decide if we did the right thing. Each time I went on duty, I trusted my safety to The Lord and put my life into His hands. Now that I'm retired, I do that each day even if I'm just going to the store or mowing the lawn. He sure takes a lot of the worry out doing a dangerous job and out of everyday living, too. All in all, I had a safe and enjoyable career as a Tennessee Wildlife Officer. It wasn't all fun and games, but neither was it all a burden. Much like most other careers, I'm sure. I made a lot of good friends and, hopefully, not too many folks thought that I was unfair to them. I guess it's a blessing to get to spend thirty years doing something you enjoy. Sorta takes most of the work out of it. But now it's time to finish these tales and go throw a stick for Cowboy, my lively Black Mouth Cur, to retrieve. I'm coming, boy, just another minute or two.

I hope you enjoy reading this book as much as I have enjoyed writing it. It was fun reliving the old times and remembering all the good sportsman that it was a pleasure to serve. I hope you gathered from reading this book that I trust The Lord as my Savior and sincerely hope you do too. Please feel free to contact me with any comments, good or bad. My e-mail address is hangin.nranch@ gmail.com. 'Till we meet again, Happy Trails and God bless!

Wildlife Officer 4309 is 10-42!

Recipes

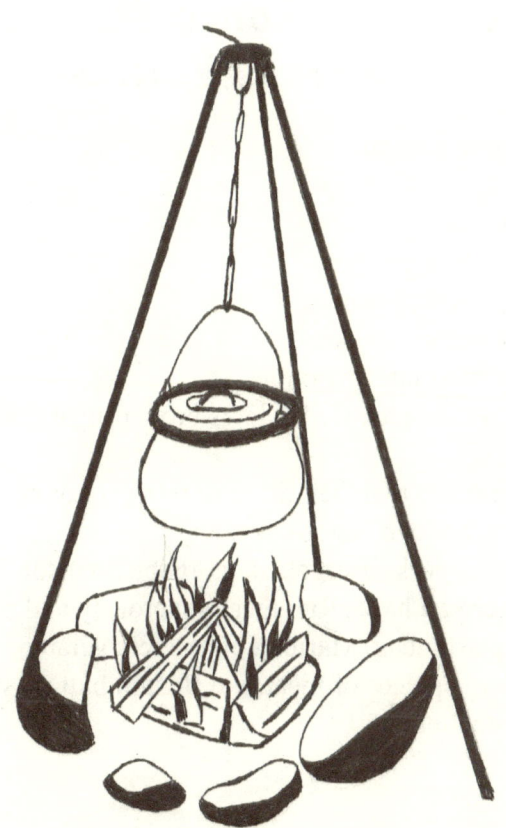

Hangin' N Ranch Meat Rub

Allen Nance, Bill Nance

1 cup light brown sugar
½ cup paprika
2 tablespoons salt
1 tablespoon black pepper
1 tablespoon garlic powder
1 tablespoon onion powder
1 tablespoon mesquite seasoning
2 packages McCormick Grill Mates brown sugar marinade

Mix all ingredients together. Store in refrigerator in a tightly sealed
   container (Zip-lock bag, Mason jar).
Rub is good for pork, beef, chicken, rabbit, venison, bear, coon,
   or whatever you have. Rub meat generously and place in heavy
   Zip lock plastic bag. Marinate in the refrigerator for about two
   days for large pieces of meat like Boston butt roast and for a day
   or so for smaller cuts.

Turtle Sauce Piquanté

Bill Nance

Roux:

1 cup oil

1 cup flour

Sauce Piquanté:

2 large onions, chopped

1 large bell pepper, chopped

3 or 4 stalks celery, chopped

5 or 6 cloves garlic, diced fine

1 eight oz. can tomato sauce

1 can diced tomatoes (I use fire-roasted)

1 package frozen cut okra

Chicken Stock

1 ½ lbs. turtle meat*

1 ½ lbs. andouille sausage (Use real Cajun andouille, if you can find it. I get mine at Coleman's Sausage and Specialty Meats in Iota, Louisiana.)

Salt to taste

Red pepper or hot pepper sauce to taste

* Crawfish, shrimp, oysters, crab, chicken, rabbit, venison, bear, or just about any kind of meat can be used. If using seafood, wait until the last 10 minutes of cooking time to add it.

To make the roux, combine the flour and oil in a large, deep cast iron skillet or Dutch oven. Stir continuously over medium-low heat until roux is the color of a milk chocolate candy bar. This will take at least an hour. You must keep stirring so it will not burn.

Add chopped onions, bell pepper, and celery. Continue to stir until onions are translucent. Add garlic, tomato sauce, and tomatoes. Cut the turtle meat into small pieces and chop or thinly slice the andouille. Add to roux mixture. Add enough chicken stock to cover and allow to simmer. Stir occasionally. Add okra, salt, and pepper. Continue to simmer and stir for a couple of hours or until you can't stand it any longer. Add more chicken stock as necessary.

Serve over hot, cooked rice with fresh garlic bread and your favorite pickles.

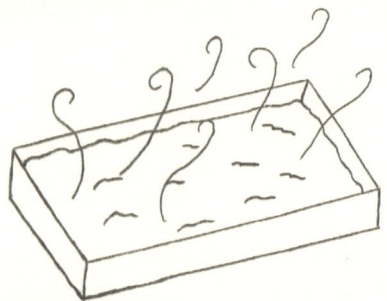

Caramel Apple Bread Pudding

Kristy Crosby, Bill Nance

1/3 cup butter, melted

1 large loaf French bread cut into 1 inch cubes
   (An electric knife works best)

1 cup Granny Smith or other tart apples, chopped

½ cup or so pecans, chopped

3 eggs lightly beaten

1 ½ cups sugar

3 cups milk

1 teaspoon cinnamon

1 teaspoon vanilla

Caramel topping (See below)

Place cubed bread into a large bowl and pour melted butter over
   the top. Add apples and pecans. Toss to mix. Combine eggs and
   sugar. Stir in milk and remaining ingredients. Pour over bread.
   When liquid is absorbed, put bread mix into a 13x9x2 glass
   baking dish and bake at 350 degrees for 45 minutes or until
   golden brown.

Caramel sauce:

1 jar real caramel sauce (Like Smucker's. Do not use caramel
   topping.)

Warm sauce over low heat until it is quite liquid. While still hot,
   add 2 teaspoons bourbon extract and quickly stir to mix. Pour
   over top of bread pudding while sauce is still hot.

Serve warm with vanilla ice cream, if desired.

Smoked Pork Shoulder
Bill Nance

1 medium to large Boston butt pork roast (10 lbs. or so)
Rub generously with Hangin' N Ranch meat rub or some other
    rub, if you must. Place in large Zip-lock bag and squeeze out
    as much air as possible. Seal bag and put into refrigerator to
    marinate for two days. Smoke at 210 degrees until internal
    temperature of the meat reaches 172-175 degrees. I use apple
    wood chips for the smoke, but other wood such as hickory or
    mesquite will work too. Keep plenty of smoke on the meat
    while cooking. You can wet the wood to make more smoke.
    This will probably take 7-8 hours, at least. Beef type meats
    like venison will be well done at 175 degrees. The meat should
    easily fall off the bone and should be easy to pull apart.
For ribs, chicken, sausage, and smaller meats, the cooking time
    will be much less. Maybe 3 hours or so. Don't overcook.
Pork ribs and Cajun boudin are great fixed this way.

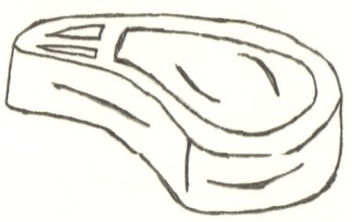

Rib Eye Steak
Bill Nance

Marinade:
¼ cup soy sauce
¼ cup Worcestershire sauce
½ cup good barbeque sauce of your choice
    (I use McCormick Brown Sugar)
Mix well
Salt and pepper steak with garlic salt and coarse black pepper.
Put steak into a Zip-lock bag and pour in marinade.
    Seal bag and refrigerate all day.
Grill on hot coals, turning frequently, and basting with the
    remaining marinade.
Cook until it's done to your liking.
Any tender steak will work; I just like rib eye.
For marinating other meats, I add a little lemon juice for fowl or a
    little brown sugar for pork.

Hot Sauce
Bill Nance

Medium hot peppers (Serrano, Jalapeno), rough chopped
Onions, rough chopped
Tomatoes, rough chopped
Use equal amounts of peppers, onions, and tomatoes
3 or 4 green onions, rough chopped
3 tablespoons vinegar per pint of sauce
1 tablespoon brown sugar per pint of sauce
2 tablespoons olive oil per pint of sauce
Garlic salt to taste
Put all ingredients into food processer and blend to desired
    consistency. You can reduce the heat a little by first removing
    the seeds from the peppers. Be sure to use rubber gloves to
    handle cut peppers.
This will be a medium to hot sauce.
Store in refrigerator in a tightly sealed container or freeze.

Sweet and Sour Slaw

1 medium head cabbage, shredded
1 medium onion, chopped
1 small bunch green onions, chopped
1 medium bell pepper, chopped
1 small jar chopped, stuffed olives
½ to ¾ cup sugar
Combine above ingredients
Dressing:
½ cup olive oil
1 cup vinegar (whatever kind you like)
1 teaspoon salt
1 teaspoon celery seed
½ teaspoon dry mustard
Combine ingredients in sauce pan and boil 3 minutes.
    Pour over cabbage mixture at once. Cover and seal tightly.
    Store in refrigerator for at least 4 hours. The longer, the better.
    It will keep up to 3 weeks.
This slaw goes great with any of the grilled or smoked meats.

TWO FARMERS—ONE WISE, THE OTHER FOOLISH

THE WISE MAN

knows the advantage of keeping game birds on his farm. He has provided for food and cover for his feathered friends. The birds have protected his crops from insects.

THE FOOLISH MAN

has left no place for the birds to stay. He has over-produced, but the cost of killing insects with poisons has taken his profit. Birds would have saved him.

Department of Game and Fish

STATE OF TENNESSEE   *March 15, 1939*

DAMON HEADDEN, State Game Warden   *G. W. Scott C.O.*

—YOUR COMMUNITY CAN HAVE GAME IF YOU WANT IT—

To order this book

Please contact Bill Nance

255 Timber Ridge Rd., Greeneville, TN 37743

Phone: (423) 620-2210

Email: hangin.nranch@gmail.com

Price of Book: $13.99